How to Know
If You're Really in Love

How to Know
If You're Really in Love

–really in love enough for marriage

by
Charlie W. Shedd

SHEED ANDREWS AND McMEEL, INC.
Subsidiary of Universal Press Syndicate
KANSAS CITY

Library of Congress Cataloging in Publication Data

Shedd, Charlie W
  How to know if you're really in love.

  1. Mate selection. 2. Marriage compatibility tests.
3. Love. I. Title.
HQ734.S534   301.41'43   78-9965
ISBN 0-8362-2803-0

Contents

Is There Any Way to Be One Hundred Percent Sure?

"What do you think of our chances?"

"Does this sound like a good bet for marriage?"

"He is just great in so many ways, but—"

"I have always thought this was the real thing, only lately . . .

"Now you have heard how it is. Do you believe we could make it?"

"We've gone so far now, we feel we ought to get married. However—"

Exact quotations from letters coming my way and all wanting to know what Janice wants to know:

Dear Dr. Shedd:

Terry and I have been going together for over a year now and he keeps asking me to marry him. He really is great in so many ways, and I don't know what's the matter, but somehow I can't make up my mind. Is there any way a girl can be one hundred percent sure so that she never ever doubts? Please can you help me decide?

Janice

Wish I could, but should anyone ever try to be one hundred percent sure? I doubt it. Those who say they are absolutely certain, with never a look back, may have turned their brains off. They could be living on emotion, minus intellect. So the goal is to begin at fifty-one percent surety, then build that to seventy-five, eighty-five, ninety.

Love is of many kinds:

Joannie and Tim are best friends. They can talk for hours about music, movies, TV personalities. They even share a common interest in the history of theater. Joannie writes: "When we first met, I really fell for Tim, hard. You know what I mean? Only now after two years, I know this interest is the only thing between us and there will never be anything more."

Greg and Cindy had a terrific reaction almost immediately. All physical. They've been dating for nine months and the only thing which has grown during this period is their first chemistry. Greg says, "Sex feelings? Wow! But when we're honest, we both know that's about all we have."

8

Debbie is an eighth grader. She's a normal junior higher, lots of friends, no great student, but she gets by. She writes: "Dear Dr. Shedd, do you think a girl can really be in love at fourteen? My father laughs at me and says it is only puppy love. How can I make him understand that Andy and I really love each other? My folks have always told me I couldn't start dating until I'm fifteen. I will be fourteen in three months, but Andy is fifteen now, and what will happen if I can't date him? So that is why I'm writing you, because I would like to make my parents understand."

Jan is a widow. Two children. Good job. Beautiful in every way. She and Louis have been spending considerable time together: bicycling, playing tennis, dinner and dancing, singing in the same choir. Yet in this one paragraph Jan makes it clear she's wondering. "Louis and I have so much in common, and I have tried to make myself believe this is the real thing. But sometimes I wake up at night thinking, where is the spark? Some way it just isn't there, no matter how hard I try. Louis says he loves me, and I can honestly say I love him some ways; but when we say it, I think he means the real thing, while I am talking about something much more casual."

Love is friendship
   Love is long conversations on the phone
      Love is sex
Love is two people laughing together, playing together
   Love is an older couple enjoying each other's
   company
      Love is a junior high crush

9

All these can be labeled love. But from here on when we use "really in love," we mean marriageable love. Is this, or is it not, a good prospect for long term building together? Does our relationship have enough ingredients for the right mix?

So how do we know? Is it the real thing? How can we be sure?

The rest of this book consists of ten major areas for testing, for thinking through. For each area we have developed a questionnaire. You will find these questionnaires in the Appendix beginning on page 123. We have duplicated the questionnaires in order that you and your friend may work them independently. Some are for judging yourself. Others are for judging your friend. The real value of these questionnaires comes when you compare answers and discuss.

Transparency: to see through; willingness to be seen; to be open; to share the inner self.

1

The Transparency Test

Dear Dr. Shedd:

If you could see Brent, you would agree he is the greatest. He has dark eyes that look straight through you. He is the star of our hockey team and lots of my friends think I am lucky to go with him. He also has great hands, if you know what I mean. In fact, sometimes I almost get carried away. But he won't talk. This makes him so mysterious, because I keep wondering what's inside, like what is he really thinking.

I have told him he is driving me wild by his silence, but it doesn't make any difference. What I am beginning to think is that Brent actually wants to keep some distance between him and other people. Do you think I am right? Is there anything I can do? You might not believe this, but sometimes I feel more lonesome when we are together than when I'm alone.

Kathy

Welcome to the club, Kathy. There are literally millions just like you. Only some are stuck with it, because they married the stranger.

The sad thing about these barricaded relationships is not what's wrong. It's what they're missing. Why? Because there is no trip to anywhere more exciting than two people traveling the inner roads in their relationship. Among the most beautiful words in our language are a man and woman saying to each other:

"I want to know you. I want you to know me."

Because this kind of total knowing is a lifetime process, it is important that anyone even thinking of marriage should ask:

"Does my friend* really want to be transparent?"

"Do I?"

Checking is important early because of the very nature of transparency. We may reveal ourselves to each other today, but tomorrow there will be more to reveal. Every door we open leads to another room with another door to open. All this takes time. It takes time to learn how. It is also scary.

Brent may he afraid. Did he grow up in a home where people lived on the surface? Where they only talked about superficial things? Where they did not trust each other? Maybe he's thinking, "If I show her who I am, and she doesn't like it, what do I have left?"

That wall around him is probably a build-up of his defenses. I wouldn't turn him off until I had tried every possible means of getting through. But you must

---

Throughout this book we use the word "friend" to mean prospect for marriageable love. "Friend" means different things to different people, but here the meaning will cover "sweetheart," "fiance," "steady," or any relationship where two people are considering a life-long commitment.

remember this too—the key to complete transparency is inside us. That's true for Brent, for Kathy, for every living person. The human doorknob only turns from inside.

THADDAEUS

We were in a Southern cafeteria. Martha (my wife) and I had gone there to meet a college girl who called long distance. She had a serious problem and wondered if she could see us. Because of her schedule and ours, we decided to meet her halfway, and I'm glad we did.

We met Thaddaeus. He was very tall, obviously somebody's basketball player. This particular chain of eating places is prone to hire college athletes.

As he was placing our food on the table, I noticed his nameplate. This was the first time I had ever seen it on a nameplate, so I said, "Thaddaeus, I've never known anyone named Thaddaeus. It's from the Bible, and it's a beautiful name."

He smiled at me, set down the tray he was holding, stood up to all six-eight of his black frame and said, "I, sir, am a beautiful person."

Someone could say that and leave a negative feeling. Others could say it and give the impression, "Good, good, all good!" That's how Thaddaeus came on.

When we had finished our meal and I was headed for the cash register, here came Thaddaeus. This time he had empty trays, so I stopped him. I thought he should know how much it meant to our friend to hear someone her age say, "I am a beautiful person." Once again he stood up to every inch of himself and said, "Sir, if you knew me like I know me, you would think I am beautiful too."

So many questions I would like to ask Thaddaeus. Who told him he was beautiful? Was it his coach? A teacher? Parents? His minister? Girl friend? Whoever convinced him of that truth did a good thing. And I would like to pass that feeling on to you.

You are a beautiful person. Inside you there is a wonderful self. Sure, there may be parts you don't like; things you've done; memories; wrong decisions you've made. Some of your actions and reactions bother you. But then there are times when you're "up" on you. You did a good thing, said the right word, struggled your way through to the moment when you could honestly say, "Nice going!"

Which is the real you?

Basically are you more bad than good? More good than bad? What about other people? In human nature is there more negative than positive? Or vice versa?

The Bible says, "It is amazing how you are together." If you accept this, then you have an excellent starting place for transparency—

The Divine creation in me is worth sharing
The Divine creation in my friend is worth knowing.

Can you also add to that belief this further premise? God made male and female with native longing to relate. Anyone who will accept that too has arrived at the beginning point for a love without limits.

16

BUT DON'T TRY TO RUSH IT

I Corinthians 13 has been called the most beautiful combination of words ever written on love. Every couple does well to read it often. And we do well to note too that there is only one repetition. This is the single four-word phrase, "We know in part."

So Brent is mysterious? Nothing the matter with that, up to a point. A touch of mystery in any man, every woman, is a good thing. Can you see your friend this way? Islands to explore, mountains to climb, rivers to travel.

Some people bore us. They lack excitement. Too shallow. Nothing beneath the surface. No more to know. Someone else may blend with them, but for us, this relationship has no future.

In marriageable love we know we have a good thing going, but part of the good thing is challenge. The spirit of this love is not, "Knowing each other completely we have a right to be married." Rather the sound here is, "We see so much yet to know, we will give the rest of our lives to knowing it."

So the tone of marriage at its best is:

We are setting out to find—
who we are
and
what we are.
We are on our way
to discover the amazing mystery
of Divine creation
in each other
and in our love.

AFFIRMATIONS FOR A LOVING LISTENER

Thirty-nine years of learning to communicate in depth have taught me some things I think might be worth passing on. I wish someone had given them to me early in our relationship. So here are my:

Affirmations for a Loving Listener

1. I will try to concentrate on what you are saying. I will train myself to put my work aside, the paper aside, anything aside and turn off what I'm thinking to focus on your words.

2. I will try to feel what you are feeling. This may be hard, but I will sincerely make the effort to get behind your words and experience what is in your heart.

3. I will give you a chance to say it all. I will hold my tongue and not comment too soon.

4. I will try to prime your pump. I will ask questions. Sometimes I will say back to you what you have said until we both understand fully what you mean.

5. If I feel even the smallest anger from you toward me, I will try my best to control my fire.

6. I will not cop out by giving no answer when an answer is important. I will remember that silence is sometimes effective, but sometimes it's cowardly.

7. When you are hurting because you're down on yourself, I will assure you again that no matter what you think of you, I am still *up* on you.

In the Appendix we have included questionnaires for your further testing of marriageable love. See page 125 for the Transparency Questionnaire.

Liberty: to liberate;
to give elbow room sufficient
for individual growth.

2

The Liberty Test

Dear Dr. Shedd:

What makes a person so jealous? That is the only thing I don't like about Tony. He is so great in every way, except he gets furious if I talk to another boy or even if another boy talks with me. I mean like on the telephone. He also doesn't like it when I go out alone with my girl friends. He says this will all get better after we're married, so I shouldn't worry. But I do, because I feel like he isn't willing to admit there is anything wrong. Am I being too suspicious? Do you think he's right that it will get better? And what can I do until then?

Teresa

Teresa is wise to be asking these questions. Why? Because emotional problems do not improve by the mere act of marriage. People only recover from whatever is bothering them when they will admit something is bothering them. Always that is true for others. Always that is true for us.

Unless Tony recognizes that he has a jealousy problem, unless he is willing to do something about it himself or let someone help him, marriage to Tony could be absolutely awful.

An anonymous grandmother has written some pensive thoughts on this theme. She is answering a girl named Gracie, because I had printed Gracie's letter in a newspaper column. Gracie was asking for help with a big decision. Gracie's life, she said, was becoming a real hell from her struggles with her suspicious husband. Was there any way out? Would this get better with the passing of time?

Now this word of response from the grandmother. This is how she saw it:

Dear Gracie:

Your letter touched me very much, so much I felt moved to write. I know what you're talking about and in my experience marriage never gets better with a jealous man. It only gets worse.

As time goes on he will become increasingly jealous, he will stifle you, criticize you, and finally if you let him, he will keep you almost a prisoner to his suspicions.

If you have children, he will resent them. He will be jealous of the time you must spend with them. He will never want you to see anyone or do anything which doesn't include him. Since he won't permit you to go out alone, he will even work overtime to keep you isolated. Then if you go against his wishes, he will vent his anger on your defenseless children. You will begin to protect your children, so things will get worse.

Nobody can say when to quit a marriage, but I can

tell you for sure what it is like to suffer a long time with a man who refuses to face facts and refuses to get help.

OTHER MISERY MAKERS

If you could put your ear down to the voices in my mail, you would know that jealousy isn't the only problem which won't get better because somebody marries it . . .

violent temper
excessive moodiness
perfectionism
drinking too much
compulsive drive for success
super stinginess
and the list goes on.

Each of these character flaws creates its own particular kind of hell. But jealousy unchecked is especially sinister, because it is the exact opposite of great love.

LET FREEDOM RING

The spirit of love at its best is "Let freedom ring." Within the framework of good marriage there will be plenty of room for each to move around, to grow individually, to develop a healthy independence.

From all over the land come the echoes:

"Gerald is so bossy that sometimes I call him 'the dictator.' This makes him mad, but he goes on doing it. He tells me what he wants me to wear and how I should do my hair. And when we go to a restaurant, he even wants to decide what I am going to eat."

"I was in the army for a while and believe me, my

wife would have made a good top sergeant. I'm telling you, almost every day I get the feeling she is shouting, 'Hup two, three, four' for everybody in our family.''

"It's so hard to live with someone who is always right. Karl will never admit that he ever made a mistake or that he was even a little bit wrong. So unless I agree with him, or do things his way, we have trouble. Can you imagine how closed in you feel married to someone like Karl?''

What's wrong with these relationships? The major wrong is that they have forgotten this basic premise:
"Each of us is here as divinely as any one of us is here.''
Those words are only one line from a long-gone poet, but the wise couple knows what he means. And they live by it, in many ways. . . .

IN THE SELECTION OF FRIENDS

Jennifer and Tommy have been married seven years. They admit that at first they tended to stifle each other. But now Jennifer says, "Sure we have some mutual friends, a lot of them, good friends. But we also have our personal friends.''

Tommy adds, "It has gone a lot better for us since we quite trying to feel the same way about everybody. Why shouldn't a wife have certain people she can vibe with? And a husband too?''

IN SEPARATE ACTIVITIES

David calls himself "a nut for flea markets.'' Patsy

thinks they're Dullsville, but they've worked out a great thing for their relationship. On Saturday afternoon he goes to flea markets while she plays tennis with her friends.

Wise couples, Jennifer and Tommy, David and Patsy, and all other lovers who have learned to say:
Within the framework of our love
   there will be plenty of room to move around.
We do not marry to reform each other,
   or to fence each other in.
We expect our relationship to change us
   for the better, together.
But we believe we will both be better
   individually and with each other
If we live in the spirit of the ancient sage:
   Let there be spaces in our togetherness.

For the Liberty Questionnaire see Appendix.

Unselfishness: getting self out of the way; concentrating on the feelings of another; caring.

3

The Unselfishness Test

Dear Dr. Shedd:

Corliss is something else. All the guys want to go with Corliss. Well, I finally landed a date, and I want to tell you what happened, because I have a question. She asked me to drive her to a town thirty miles away. So of course, I did. Then when we got there, we ended up at a disco, and here comes the bad part. There was this guy waiting to meet her. So she gave me a sob story about what a terrible problem he had, and would it be all right if she rode back home with him.

You get it, don't you? They had this all decided ahead of time, but what else could I do? Now this is what I want to know. Is there any way you can tell if someone is just using you?

Ron

Very hard to tell for sure, Ron. So charge this one to experience, and be glad it happened before you really got hooked. Most manipulators are much more subtle than Corliss. Sometimes it can even take years to catch on. And if all the victims of these con artists were to say "Amen," their sound would be heard round the world.

You are right when you say, "Corliss is something else." What she is, is very risky material for a good marriage. In a good marriage, the predominant spirit is not, "What will you do for me?" but "What can I do for you?"

I wish I could give you a two-sided scale for all your relationships where you could put selfishness on one side and unselfishness on the other. Then you could see if they balanced well. But since there is no such scale, it's smart to keep checking.

"D" LOVE, "B" LOVE

One of the most helpful measuring concepts for me is the "D" Love, "B" Love theory. I first heard it presented when I was on the board of a psychiatric hospital. For eight years I listened to these doctors of the mind read their papers. Some of them were much too involved for me, but others were right on target. And this one came through loud and clear.

"All love," this psychiatrist said, "can be divided in two parts: 'D' Love and 'B' Love."

"D" Love stands for "Deficits."

"B" Love is for "Being."

In "D" love, we are loving, because of deficits in us.

Why do we fall in love? There must be almost as many reasons as there are people, but I know one reason I fell in love. Very soon after I met Martha, I discovered she had in her a deep quiet which I very much needed.

I came from a background of constant uproar, and I thought everyone in the world lived like our family. "Is anyone calm around here? Let's fuss and fret and give him the jitters."

Then my path crossed Martha's path and I knew what the Bible meant by those magnificent words, "He leadeth me beside still waters."

At first I couldn't believe anyone in the world was really like this from the inside. But all the time I think I had been looking, hoping, waiting; and when I found it, I knew this was for me.

Is it wrong to marry someone because that someone has what you need? No way, provided you can meet that person's need with what you have.

Were you to ask Martha, "What need has Charlie met for you?" I'm certain one quality she'd mention is "confidence." I've always been blessed with an abundance of "I can do it" . . . "We can do it" . . . "Let's do it." She had seldom heard these words over the road she'd come.

So from where we are today, both of us would say there is nothing wrong with deficit love when it's a healthy part of the relationship.

The same for dating. Betsy explains:

Ben came into my life at just the right time. I had been hurt very bad and what I needed was someone to pick me up. Well, Ben is such a good listener, and so understanding, but actually all he is to me is like a big brother. He knows it, and I will tell you something

31

else. He isn't in love with me either and I know that.

At the beginning of this year Ben didn't know anyone in our school, because his family had just moved here. So I have been able to show him around and help him meet a lot of people, and tell him some things to make it easier.

When you both know what you are doing and you are honest, don't you think it's all right to date because you need each other?

It's not only all right, Betsy. It's great, and your key word here is "honesty."

When Corliss gives Ron a date for transportation without telling him the whole story, this girl is bad news. But when we have found someone who can build on our deficits to make us better people, this is good, good news.

"B" LOVE

"B" love says, "I love you because you are. I love you because you exist."

The big label for this kind of love is "unselfishness." Even if your love starts on the "D" level and you both know it, you really haven't arrived at marriageable love until the "B" aspect begins to dominate. So the question is: On each side is there a gradual moving away from "me, me, me" to "you, you, you"?

SIGNS THAT WE ARE MOVING TOWARD "B" LOVE

"I LIKE YOU BECAUSE"

How often do you compliment each other? When

was the last time one of you, without prompting, said a good word? I mean about the other person, to the other person, unexpected?

For thirty-nine years Martha and I have lived by this agreement:

Every day at least once we will say to each other,

"I like you because . . ."

Our favorite term for this little deal is the psychological expression, "warm fuzzy."

Sometimes we forget. It may be one of those days we've both been busy. Hardly saw each other; too many people around; or we were thinking only of ourselves. So sometime late in the evening, bedtime, she will say, "Charlie, I haven't had my warm fuzzy." Or I might tell her I haven't had mine.

Sounds like a game? It is, a fun game. But for us it's much more than a game. It's a way of being certain that our relationship moves continually in the direction of "B" love.

Do we pay each other the same old compliments?

Sure, sometimes. But I can't think of one occasion when either of us ever said, "You told me that before." The truth is that every son of Adam and every daughter of Eve is put together in the original to appreciate appreciation.

If this sounds like a possibility for you, here's a word of advice about "sameness": Keep putting the old accolades in new words. Fresh touches have a way of making previous compliments acceptable over and over.

This would never do for you? Artificial? Too structured? Before you turn it off, could you manage a "warm fuzzy" agreement for thirty days? We have recommended our practice to countless couples, and countless couples have told us this simple little procedure has done wonders for them.

THE NEW COMPLIMENT

That isn't all. Because our daily compliment came to mean so much, we decided to improve on that by paying each other a *new* compliment every week. The spirit of this one is, "I like you because I've discovered something new and wonderful about you."

When we multiply the thirty-nine years we've been married by fifty-two weeks, Martha knows more than two thousand things I like about her. And vice versa. Is it any wonder we are absolutely bananas about each other?

How can anyone find something new every week for thirty-nine years? The reason it's possible is that the more you look for good, the more good there is to see.

How long would it take to run out of positives?

Vignette from a recent marriage workshop in Texas:

Our opening banquet was attended by dating couples, newly marrieds, middle-aged, and some very old. This event was followed next morning by a seminar on "Communication at Its Best." We had hardly begun when an elderly lady asked for the floor, came to the podium and said:

"If you were at the banquet last night, you know we were asked before we went to bed to think up something new we liked about each other.

"Now dad and I have been married sixty-two years and while we were watching the late news, I asked

34

myself, 'Is there anything I like about him I haven't told him?' Then all of a sudden it came to me that Frank has nice ears. You know what I mean? Some people have ears too big, some too small, some sort of funny looking, but his are just right. So I told him, 'I like your ears, Frank.' Well, I want to tell you we had a lot of fun over that."

"B" love, in its highest form, takes years to accomplish. It is an art to be learned, a discipline to be practiced, a goal.

Does any couple ever achieve it totally? Probably not. But those who keep their love moving in this direction are headed for the high ground of marriage at its best. And courtship is the time to begin shaping habits which can make the relationship a growing turn-on forever.

THE LITTLE EXTRAS

Words aren't the only way of moving a relationship from "D" love to "B" love. Here's another test. How many things do you *do* for each other which are not necessary, but nice?

> A student nurse:
> "Do you know what I like about Roger? It is that he sometimes surprises me with little things which let me know he's thinking of me. I will give you an example. One day last week he brought me this little package of tissues for cleaning my glasses. You see I wear thick glasses and it seems like they are always steaming over or smudgy. So when he gave them to me, he said, 'I saw them by the checkout

counter at the drug store and they made me think of you.' "

High school senior:
"I'm on the basketball team and we had a good season, so we got a lot of publicity. But we lost in the semifinals. Of course, I wasn't feeling so good about that. But the next week Heather gave me a scrapbook which she had been making, only I didn't know she was doing it. It had all these pictures and writeups and everything. I tell you it really made me feel great."

Two little stories from two fortunate people. Fortunate, because they have met someone who at the dating level is capable of "B" love.

Now let's move on down the years and have a look at the same thing in marriage.

"I think I am the luckiest woman in the world. Harry and I have been married seventeen years and every week when I clean the house, he runs the vacuum sweeper for me. Do you know how many husbands do that?"

"Do you know what my wife did last week? She called me at the office at ten o'clock, asked me if I had a date for lunch. Then when I told her I didn't, she said, I'm going to pack a picnic and I'll meet you in the park. I miss you, and I want to be with you.' Now isn't that something? Just this morning at coffee one of my friends said his wife was always griping that she never gets to see him. Well, why doesn't she pack a picnic?''

"Gene is in a high-pressure job and most of the time when he comes home, I can tell he has had it. But some days I have had it too, and I don't think I could ever tell you what it means when he says, 'Elsie, you go have a hot bath, I'll take the kids to the playground.' Of course, he doesn't do this often, just every now and then. But I tell you what a woman appreciates is someone who cares enough to notice when she's down.''

Myriad and infinite are the little bits of love which come from that magic ingredient of an unselfish spirit. But many foolish couples let the little extras slip away. They take it for granted that because they said "we do," they also said, "We've done it." The fact is that our need for "B" love does not diminish as the years go by. It increases. The wise couple goes on forever saying by word and action:

"I appreciate what you are doing for me, but even more, thanks for being you."

WARNING

There is a form of praise which is nothing more than

"chattery-flattery." Some of these geysers of "Oh, aren't you wonderful" almost mesmerize us. We are awed that we could be so "marvelously marvelous." Then comes the shadowy truth that this is an act and we are victims of a real "D" phony. These characters are not enamored of us, they are enamored of themselves enamoring us.

One girl sums it up like this: "You mean D love is sort of like my cat. She doesn't rub against me, because she likes me. She does it because it makes *her* feel good."

In the original the word "sincere" comes from two words meaning "without wax." That expression has an interesting history. In the marketplace when a potter would damage one of his vessels, he might, if he were clever enough, cover the crack with wax. Then he would glaze it over and sell it for first quality. So the term "without wax" came to mean "genuine." No cover up. The real thing. Sincere.

Say it again: marriageable love does not ask for a finished product. The important ingredient is potential for growing into a genuine "I love you because you're you" relationship.

See Appendix for the Unselfishness Questionnaire.

Mercy: not judgmental;
quality of compassion;
forgiving.

The Mercy Test

I wish I could sit down with every Debbie and Susan, all the Becky's and Janet's, the Billy's and Bob's who have written me about their mistakes, asking what they can do now. Hundreds, thousands of almost every name, from the deep places inside, are hoping they might someday meet someone with whom they can share:

> where they have been weak
> things they've done wrong
> their uglies, negatives, sins.

For marriageable love there must be a large measure of mercy. Here are some letters pointing to the most delicate nuances of "how much to tell" and "how to accept what's told."

LETTER # 1

"IS IT ALL RIGHT NOT TO TELL SOME THINGS?"

Dear Dr. Shedd:
Please can you help me? I don't know what to do.

Doug and I are going to be engaged on my birthday
and I love him more than anything. What worries me is
that I am wondering how much you should tell each
other, and is it all right not to tell some things?

I don't like to say it, but the truth is I am ashamed of
what happened in junior high. I was very immature
and so lonesome. If only I could begin over again. I
have never said anything to Doug or anybody about
this part of my life. I guess it's because I'm afraid.
What if he wouldn't like me as much? I have thought
about it and even tried sometimes to tell him. But I get
so scared. Do I have to tell? Is it all that important for
a person to know all about the one he is going to
marry?

Love,
Elizabeth

No, Elizabeth, you don't
have to tell. Or at least not
until you have asked yourself
some very important
questions about Doug, and
about you, and the two of you
together.

Is Doug the kind of person
you would describe as
merciful? Have you seen
signs in him which would
indicate a forgiving spirit? Is
he tolerant of others, kind in
the things he says about
them? Does he recognize his
own faults?

And are you the type who can be satisfied with something other than togetherness all the way? Are you one of those people who can accept forgiveness from God without going through another person?

A famous psychiatrist says, "No individual can know complete peace until he has surfaced himself totally to one other person." So he goes on to advise that any couple considering marriage should put it all out on the table right now.

I don't agree. In the first place I have known some good marriages where they didn't tell each other everything before they were married, or after. Then too in the best marriages, they understand that complete surfacing is a goal, a pilgrimage. Sometimes it's a fun trip, sometimes it isn't. Sometimes it's embarrassing, sometimes awful.

For Doug and Elizabeth and every couple asking

these questions, it is all
important to have some
agreements before marriage:
"If we decide we will not tell
all, then we will not rummage
around in our indiscretions;
we will bury the past; we will
accept the forgiveness of
God, and *shut up!*"

LETTER # 2

"SHE'S A BLOODHOUND FOR ERROR"

Suffering husband:

My wife is a bloodhound for error. She has an uncanny nose for even the smallest trace of somebody doing wrong. And when she gets on the trail, you can bet she's going to be baying loud and long and never letting up. I should know, because most of the time she makes me feel like a criminal. And I tell you it is awful, just awful! Actually, she's always been like this and I guess the worst part is, she never forgets.

In one of its most beautiful chapters on love, the Bible says, "Love keeps no record of wrongs."

Consider the difference between the baying woman and one line from another couple:

"Whenever either of us has blown it and said, It was my

fault; when we have talked about it and settled it; then we put it on the shelf and tomorrow is a new beginning."

So why aren't more couples living by some such credo? One answer is that many of these record keepers are suffering from exaggerated guilt of their own. They frantically follow other tracks to keep from turning inward.

I've worked with enough "bloodhounds for error" to know that many times what they need is to forgive themselves. And until they do they will be unpleasant for other people to live with, but also they will be in miserable company even when they are alone.

And how can you tell whether you might one day be the victim of this "awful, just awful"?

Here's one answer:

LETTER # 3

"HE ALWAYS TRIES TO GET BACK AT PEOPLE"

"There is this one thing which bothers me about Eddy. It is the way he always tries to get back at people, even people he barely knows, or maybe he doesn't know them at all.

For instance, when he is driving, he gets furious when someone cuts in ahead of him. So right away it's as if he is thinking of them as the enemy. Then he speeds up to get around them again, and I know someday we're going to have an accident. He does the same thing in other situations too. Actually, he hasn't done it all that much with me, but I am beginning to ask myself how much of this can I stand?

Keep asking, because you are right on target to a possible future problem. You say he hasn't done it all that much with you. I'm glad he hasn't. But I think you would be wise to add the one word "yet."

Here is a tricky little maneuver which some lovers develop before marriage:

During courtship, when they are together they manage to keep their negatives in check. But after marriage the strain is too much, and they open fire on their closest target. I have seen this often enough to say that hostility of every kind should be checked, double-checked, and checked again.

Is your friend angry at anyone? Or anything? If the answer is yes, the fury may one day change direction and come down all over you.

Here we are again at the all-important question: Do you like the way your friend treats other people?

LETTER # 4

"I LOVE YOU FOR WHAT YOU ARE"

Divorcee planning her second marriage:

You might as well know the truth. My first marriage ended because of things I did wrong. When I met Aaron, I knew that he knew, and it bothered me terribly. Then when we began to get serious, I told him there were certain matters we probably should discuss. Do you know I could hardly believe it when he said, "Alison, I don't care where you have been or what you have done. I love you for what you are right now and for what we can be together."

I nominate this for one beautiful letter, beautiful because Aaron's words are echoes of God's mercy in its highest form. This is what theologians call "Grace" and they define it as "the free unmerited love and favor of God." Touches of that are all-important for marriageable love, and developing it to the fullest measure takes a lifetime.

That is why I'd like to sit down with each Debbie and Susan, Becky and Janet, Billy and Bob, and hundreds and thousands of almost every name. And if I could, I would say, "Keep testing until you are sure there is a good measure of mercy in this relationship. And I hope someday you will find someone like Aaron who will tell you,

> "I love you for what you are right now and for what we can be together."

In a love like this you can relax. Nothing to fear. Nothing to hide. Nothing to do but accept this love, enjoy, and pass it on to others standing in the need of grace.

Apology: willingness to admit wrong; to regret mistakes and say so.

The Apology Test

Dear Dr. Shedd:

Does it really matter if the girl you are thinking about marrying cannot tell you she is sorry? I mean like something happens between you and it is her fault. You know it, but you also know she is never going to admit it. So you have to work it around to get it back together, because you don't want it to go on the way things are.

Then you go ahead and say you're sorry when she should be the one. You really kind of regret it now since you don't feel so good about yourself.

What makes a girl this way? Can you tell me if I am worrying too much about something not all that important?

Gary

No, you aren't worrying
too much. The sounds of
"forgive me, I'm sorry, I was
wrong" are an absolute must

51

for marriageable love. And for the emotional health of both parties, they must be heard from both sides.

In the movie *Love Story* and the book of that title there is one sentimental line which has become something of a proverb—

"Love is never having to say you're sorry."

Only one thing wrong with that platitude. *It is not true!* If you think it could be, read on.

From Pamela, pondering a future with Gordon:

"Gordon never admits he has made a mistake. Sometimes he tries to show it by being extra nice, but I've never one time heard him say that anything was his fault. I have talked to him about this, and I don't think I'm getting through. Some way it is just as if something won't let him say, 'I'm sorry.'"

From Dorothy, after thirteen years of marriage:

"The way my husband acts you'd think he wrote the Ten Commandments. If anything goes wrong, even if he had a part in it, he blames me, the children, the neighbors, or somebody in Washington. I tell you for sure, people like him are no fun to live with."

Pamela has analyzed the situation right. She isn't

getting through, and the odds are anything but favorable. Most of these characters are impervious to help from anyone close. Reason? They pounce on every small flaw in the people they live with, and then they do what Dorothy's husband does. They project. Always they put the blame on someone else.

Grim statistic: I cannot think of a single situation where one of these rigid personalities learned to unbend without professional help. And because they refuse to consider even the remote possibility they could be wrong, there is very little possibility of getting them to professional help. So whenever you hear these phrases, and others like them, you can be sure this is the sound of distant thunder:

"It's your fault" . . . "If only you would change" . . . "You're the one who should see a psychiatrist."

Is Gary's girl hung up somewhere in her background? Probably. Ditto for Gordon, for Dorothy's husband, and the whole stiff-necked parade of non-apologizers.

When they were children did they need to over-defend themselves? Did someone exaggerate their mistakes, laugh at them, hold them up for the crowd's derision? Was punishment so severe in their homes that they lied to protect themselves? And were they afraid of the truth because of the consequences?

Gary's letter is unusual in this respect. Most often it is the woman writing, because her man doesn't apologize. But there may be an additional reason when the man won't say he's sorry. Perhaps it's a matter of "maleness." Someone, somehow made an impression on the growing boy that to admit wrong was not manly. But could the very opposite be true?

From a son, fourteen:
"You know what I really like about my dad which is different from most of my friends' dads? My dad will say, 'Don't ever be afraid to admit you're wrong. You'll feel better. Besides you couldn't be perfect, because your dad isn't. Always remember son, it takes a real man to admit he's wrong.' I tell you it is great to live with someone who knows he is not perfect, because then you don't have to worry all that much."

"YOU'LL FEEL BETTER"

Those three words "you'll feel better" are also worth a replay, and another.

When you are being stubborn you actually do feel better if you come down off your righteousness.

I said that I cannot think of a single case where one of these rigid personalities could learn to unbend without professional help. But I have known a few who were helped a little when they picked up bits of this sound:

Maybe, just maybe, you would respect yourself more if you would humble yourself to apologize. So keep saying it:

"I would think more of you
The people at work would think more of you
Your children would think more of you
The whole world would think more of you
You would think more of yourself
If just one time you could say,
I'm sorry."

TRUE HUMILITY

Meekness is a beautiful Biblical word which has lost most of its meaning in false connotation. When we think of "meek," we picture "Timid Soul" standing on the corner in a driving rain, saying in shaky voice, "If that guy doesn't come in another forty-five minutes, he can just go borrow the money from somebody else."

But this is one hundred and eighty degrees around the circle from true meekness. To be meek in the Biblical sense is to know the difference between what we are and what we were meant to be.

And meekness in this sense has a beautiful ring. It is

beautiful to live with, beautiful for other people, beautiful to feel in our own hearts.

How do we get it?
Step one:
We believe God made us; He has a purpose for us; and there is a distinct possibility that we haven't lived up to His original dream.

Step two:
We accept the fact that God accepts us even when it's hard for us to accept ourselves. He understands. He knows our faults. He loves us in spite of them. Small wrongs, big wrongs, He still loves us, still accepts us.

When we believe in a God like that and accept His love, then we can accept ourselves and say, "I too am *sometimes wrong*!"

THE PHONY

Did you ever meet a person who was so self-righteous he turned you off? Or she did?

These we have with us always. The pious souls who mistake themselves for God The Father Almighty. Here's one:

"My husband never entertained even a flickering thought that he could be anything other than one hundred percent right one hundred percent of the time. And would you believe this man is a preacher?

"Since he is always quoting the Bible, I keep quoting back to him, '*All* have sinned and come short of the glory of God.' Result? Zero. He won't buy it where it applies to him. Do you know what I think is the matter? I think he doesn't know the difference between himself and God.''

If you are considering marriageable love to someone who has even minor shadings of such pomposity, the line for you is:

"No one is perfect, friend,
and you aren't.
I can see myself
growing weary
doing all the repair work myself.
So unless you can learn to admit
when you're wrong,
        I'm moving on.''

See questionnaire for Mercy-Apology in the Appendix.

Sexuality: passionate urges; desire to be physically intimate; the God-given drive to reproduce, but even more to enjoy the ecstasy of bodily union.

6

The Sexuality Test

Questions, questions, dozens of questions. Hundreds. Thousands. From college and university, high schoolers, and the junior high. Singles out there working now. The divorced, widowed, widowers too. From all of these a barrage of questions on sex.

They come by letter.*

They also come by written slip, on 3 x 5 card, notebook sheets, scraps of paper. This is dialogue time at conference, bull session, seminar, rally. I once heard a precocious young listener say (about his preacher), "He's O.K., I guess, but he spends too much time answering questions nobody ever asks."

---

*Dr. Shedd has written extensively in the field of sex and dating, courtship, love, and marriage. He has been the author of a popular Sex and Dating column in one of America's leading youth magazines. His book, The Stork is Dead, has drawn thousands of letters from teenagers. In addition, his two books on marriage, Letter to Karen and Letters to Philip, both million sellers, have brought countless queries from the married and those considering marriage. All these provide the background for this chapter.–Editor

That would be an easy trap for me too, so whenever I am speaking to high schoolers, the college set and young singles I begin my presentations with the simple statement:

"What would you like to ask someone who has heard from thousands of people like you?

"When it comes to love, marriage, sex, dating, I have a file drawer full of any situation you can describe. I know every possible problem you could get into in the back seats of cars; up in Susie's room when the folks aren't home; the beach; the motel. Anywhere two bodies are in close proximity, I know what might happen; what does happen.

"I am not here to judge you, or to put you down. I have my beliefs and they mean everything to me. I will tell you what they are and I hope you will respect my right to my beliefs. I will listen to you and I will extend you the dignity of deciding what you will do.

"And no matter what you do, I will love you."

WHAT I BELIEVE

In vain we call old notions "fudge"
And seek to bend our conscience to our dealing
Yet still the Ten Commandments will not budge
And stealing yet remains but stealing.
                    Anonymous

So does adultery remain adultery, and ditto for fornication. I believe that God gave us His laws for our good. He also gave us our urges, powerful urges, but that isn't all. In addition to His laws and our urges, He gave us the wonderful gift of freedom to decide what we will do.

I do not believe that premarital sex can be sex at its best. Neither can extramarital sex, nor open marriage in the meaning of "do your own thing whenever, wherever."

The poet is right. It does not matter how we try to bend the laws. Some things remain as God ordained them. And one of these is that sex at its best is not a happening. It is a creation. It is not alone the joining of two bodies. It is the gradual coming together of two lives in their unique response to the goodness of God.

So no matter what you may have thought about sex; no matter what distortions our mistaken adult world has passed along to you; no matter how bizarre the newspaper; how painful the hurt of your own experience; I hope you can come to marriageable love believing

> sex is the most beautiful
> > coming together
> > > of any of the mysterious blendings
> > > > in God's creation.
> For rapture,
> > for wonder,
> > > for meaning,
> > > > nothing can equal sex
> > > > > when it is right.

NOW TO THE QUESTIONS

From a mountain of questions I have selected only those which apply to marriageable love. Some come from the neophyte, but many from those who are into sex. Reason? Many of the couples I know who are thinking about marriage are into sex.

Mark those which need to be discussed between the two of you.

IS SEX ENOUGH REASON FOR MARRIAGE?

"Do you think because you have had sex with a certain boy that you should marry him? I always said I would never make love with anyone except my husband. But now it has happened, and I am really not sure whether I love him, or ever did."

"The girl I am going with is nice and all that, but I don't want to marry her, because I am not ready to get married to anyone, and if I was ready, I don't think it would be her. She keeps saying that since we are having sex, we should get married. Do you think we should?"

No I don't think you should. Guilty feelings are not a good basis for marriage. If you marry from a forced sense of obligation, you'll be sorry. Two wrongs don't make a right. So what does? The only way I know to make wrong right is to turn it over to God, accept His forgiveness, and go on living His way.

SHOULD WE BE USING BIRTH CONTROL?

"We are engaged and have been going all the way. But there is one problem. He thinks we should be using birth control, and I don't like the idea, because it seems to me as if that would make it a little more wrong. I am not sure why I feel this way, but I feel it very much. Can you help us?''

Wish I could. Fast. I believe that since you have opted for sex, you must also take on yourselves the responsibility of using birth control. Run, don't walk to the nearest drug store or to someone with whom you can talk protection.

There is no such thing as "a little bit pregnant." And I weary of couples telling me, "It's our business if we have intercourse." Not true. An unplanned pregnancy draws a wide circle. It can soon become the business of parents, brothers, sisters, other relatives. It might also become the business of your school, the church, society. And your pregnancy certainly gives an unborn baby the business, doesn't it?

As if this were not enough, there is another factor which must be faced. An unplanned pregnancy may affect your own attitudes (conscious or subconscious) for years to come.

LIVING TOGETHER BEFORE MARRIAGE

"Do you believe in living together before marriage? My fiancee and I have been discussing this, and he says we should try it to see how everything goes before we get married. I suppose you have heard from other people who have done it. How did it go for them?''

There are almost as many answers as there are couples living together, and that's too many. I say "too many" because I have seen too many hurts, too many "used" feelings, too many reduced self-images, too many negatives for me to think positively of any arrangement outside marriage. Whether it is labelled "living together," "shacking up," "no strings attached," or "keeping the back door open," I cannot buy it.

I believe the greatest man-woman relationships can only be a lifetime creation of two people who will say, "I do" and not "maybe."

USED AND DUMPED

"This is very hard for me to write. But I need help right now so bad. My problem is that I gave in to my boy friend. He kept saying, 'If you loved me, you'd let me.' So I did. Then it wasn't long until he dumped me. Just like that he dumped me, and now he is with another girl. I feel so used, so ruined. I wonder if anyone will ever want to marry me."

"Used and dumped." I hear it from every state of the union. Often. And they stand in long queues to hear someone say, "You are not ruined. You are still a person of worth."

Actually you can even be a finer person than you were before this happened. God has a way of taking our hurts, and using them for good, if we let Him.

So keep your hand in the Hand of the Lord because He can lead you to someone who knows what mercy is. And it just may be that the person He leads you to will need mercy too, from you.

PREGNANT AND UNMARRIED

"I am pregnant and don't know what to do. Dale says he will marry me to give the baby a name, but I don't think he really wants to. Do you know many couples who had to get married and how did it work out for them?

Yes, I know couples who had to get married. Lots of them. Some of them are happy, some aren't. I also know some who married to give the baby a name, and life was hell. It was hell for her, because she wanted to be free for a while to live her own life. It was hell for him, because he was thinking, "Look what she did to me."

Seems so unfair? Unfair for the mother to want her freedom? Unfair for the boy to blame it on her? Unfair for the baby to not really be wanted?

Of course, it's unfair. But that's the way it is in too many unplanned pregnancies, too many "unfairs."

ABORTION

"What do you think about abortion? I am pregnant and do not want to get married. Believe me, he doesn't want to either. I have been thinking and thinking, and putting off the decision. But now the time has come for me to decide something.

"A part of me would like to keep my baby, but in my circumstances there are so many complications. When I'm thinking straight, I know my parents would have to help and is that really right for them?

"Another choice would be to give my baby up for adoption, but that seems so hard.

"Then of course there is abortion, but I am wondering if it is really right to take a life that way. You can see it is one of the biggest decisions I have ever had to make and that is why I am writing you."

You sound like such a sensitive person and I admire the way you are thinking through all the involvements. You are aware that they relate to you and other people and your baby. Especially, I admire the way you ask, "Is it right to take a life?"

I do not think it is, and for that reason I do not recommend abortion. I think every baby is a child of God at the moment of conception and because that is true I think your baby has a right to live.

You are also right about your parents. In most situations it is too heavy a burden for grandparents when they are saddled with a baby.

So let's have another look at adoption. Because we have one adopted child, I know what that can mean. Many couples today would like to adopt. That's why I think you would be doing a wonderful thing for someone else if you decide this is the way.

Above all remember God made you beautiful; you still are beautiful; and He can use everything that happens to bless you and others in His plan.

IS VIRGINITY IMPORTANT?

"This may sound strange to you, but one of my goals has always been that I would be a virgin when I got married. Because of my family background and religious training, it really does mean everything to me. My sorority sisters say this is ridiculous, because all the boys want experienced women. What do you think?"

I think your sorority sisters are listening to the boys who are pitching them for sex. But they don't all want experienced women, not for marriage. In one of my recent seminars a college student said something which gives the other side. In a quiet voice, almost as though talking to himself, he said, "When I get married, I would sure like to feel that no one else has been there ahead of me."

Ninety percent of the ones I rap with agree.

HOW FAR CAN WE GO?

"How far can we go, necking and petting, and like that and still be safe?"

This is one of the three most frequently asked questions. And ordinarily it means how far can we go without going all the way?

If we define necking as anything above the neck and petting as anything below, then here's the plain answer to "How far can we go?"

Hands outside the clothes.

The God who made us put us together so that skin against skin below the neck is much too much of a turn-on for most couples.

So what does this have to do with marriageable

love? Maybe everything. The decisions we make now, the life we live now, the way we share ourselves now; all these things do make a difference. They may make a difference as long as we live.

LENGTH OF ENGAGEMENT

"Do you have any advice on length of engagement? Our folks don't want us to get married until we have finished college and that's two years. We know we want to marry each other, so we would like to be engaged. Do you think that might be too long?

Yes, it would be too long. A very good rule for engagements is: the shorter, the better.

And here's some added advice from one who has seen too many long engagements: Ask your folks if they will sit down with you and discuss your situation. Tell them honestly how you feel, why you think you should be married, and solicit their help.

THE SEX SUBSTITUTES

"Oral sex?" . . . "Mutual masturbation?"

Adults would have the vapors if they knew how much oral sex and mutual masturbation goes on among today's young strugglers.

Sometimes these things are a part of foreplay. More often with the unmarried they are used as a form of birth control. Then some are into the substitutes for another reason. They have decided that regular intercourse would be wrong now, but somehow for them the substitutes are acceptable.

Too often the indulgers have not considered this fact: Oral intercourse and mutual masturbation can become a fixation. Most experts agree sex substitutes are a negative if they never move on to the real thing.

ANY LIMITS IN MARRIAGE?

"My boy friend and I have agreed that we will not have sex until we are married. However, we have talked a lot about sex, and there is something which bothers me. He shows me magazines and has even taken me to X-rated movies. Some of the things they do in those movies almost make me sick.

"He says, 'Don't worry. That's what you do after you're married.' Is this true? Do you have to do everything?"

No, you don't. You don't have to do anything repulsive to you. But what is repulsive to you may be a very nice thing for others. When a couple believes that everything about the body is part of Divine creation, then there are no limits. Another good rule for married sex: If it does not harm either of you physically or emotionally; if you both want to do it and you like it; it can't be wrong. God made your body to be enjoyed.

THOSE WILD FANTASIES

"Is it natural to have fantasies about other girls when you are with the one you are going to marry? Sometimes I wonder if I am the worst person on earth, because I feel so unfaithful in my head. I'm sure I'm in love, but I have even been asking myself if we should call it off until I get it straight?"

"When I was a senior in high school, I was in love with Bruce and we agreed that some day we would marry. Then he broke it up and I can tell you it was the worst thing that ever happened to me. Now I'm a junior in college and engaged to Keith. Honestly, he is everything I ever wanted, but even when we have sex, my mind goes back to Bruce. Some of the thoughts I have really worry me. Will this go on forever?"

Fantasies are a natural part of the human mental process. Almost everyone has them to some degree. So they do not mean that you are evil, only normal. The main thing is to keep them in check and the best way to do this is sharing them with the person you love. In the finest marriages I know, the spirit is, "Anything you need to talk about for your inner peace? Let's discuss it." That kind of healing intimacy is rare, but it is a great goal for marriageable love.

HE LOOKS AT OTHER GIRLS

"My fiancee is super in almost every way only he looks at other girls so much. He says he would never be unfaithful, and that it is normal. Do you think he will still do this after we are married?"

Yes, I think he will. I also think it's normal. One funny friend says: "Following the straight and narrow is O.K., but it's more exciting to follow the ones with curves."

One woman I know has helped her husband make a game of this. They live on a beach where girls parade in bikinis, they loll in bikinis, bathe in bikinis. Because she knows his preferences, they have fun *together* evaluating the various arrangements of molecules. And she talks to him about the male bodies she likes. For them it really is super and I should know, because I'm the lucky husband.

HE ISN'T INTERESTED IN SEX

"Do you think there is something funny about Ronald? We have gone together eighteen months and he has never shown any interest in sex. I hear the other girls telling about their boy friends, and I wonder. So I talked to him a couple times lately, and he says he doesn't care about that stuff. Could it be that he is all that much of a gentleman? Do you think when we get married it will be different?"

No, I don't think it will be different when you get married. No matter how much self-control you both have, after eighteen months there should be some powerful urges between you. It isn't one bit normal for a healthy boy to say he doesn't care "about that stuff." Sounds as if Ronald needs help. And if he doesn't get it, and you marry him, you'll need help. Bad!

SEX ALL THE TIME?

"I am getting married the end of next semester and I have a problem. The problem is that my boy friend talks about sex all the time. As a matter of fact, I think some days he doesn't think about anything but sex. We have discussed this, but he only laughs. He says when we are married, he won't have to talk about it all the time, because we will be doing it all the time. You may think this is a strange question, but will you please tell me, how often do married people have sex?"

It is not a strange question, I hear it regularly, but there is no single answer. Frequency patterns vary. They vary with each marriage. They also vary from time to time in any one marriage.

At first most couples are extremely active. Then it may taper off or maybe it won't. I know some happy marriages where they get by on the sparse diet of sex once a week. Then there are some sexual athletes who enjoy it daily. Average for couples I know would come out in the range of two to three times weekly.

QUANTITY OR QUALITY

"Since our engagement, my fiancee and I have been making love. This is what we decided to do. I enjoy it most of the time, but the problem is that he wants sex so much oftener than I do. Is this normal?"

Yes, it's normal. No matter what the unisexers say, there will always be delicate differences between male and female. One big difference with most couples is this: man thinks "quantity" (how often), woman thinks "quality" (how). When these two attitudes start moving toward each other, married love begins to be what it ought to be.

SOMETHING YOU PUT UP WITH?

"We are going to be married this summer and I am worried. All my life I have been taught that sex is

74

something you put up with if you are a woman. Of course, it was my mother mostly who gave me this idea. What I wonder is how do you get over that feeling?"

Let's hope your husband will be a super educator, kind and understanding. You need a man like that. I'm glad you want to get over your feelings. Of course, there are counsellors who can help you, but I doubt if you need that much help.

I know many girls who were brought up with this kind of chronic down-pull, and many of them rose above it. You will rise above it too if you and the man you marry live by this truth: Sex is a wonderful gift of a wonderful God. He wants you to let yourself go and enjoy the whole thing together.

WILL IT FIT?

Some questions, particularly out of the teen scene, seem almost ludicrous. I have trained myself to be completely unflappable with whatever comes next. I also smile inside with some of the questions and some of their own solutions. Especially this is true in "the lines guys use" and the very clear way some girls say "No."

Example:

"My boy friend says we should try it to see if it fits."

I think the best reply to this pitch comes from a super sharp girl in California. She was almost certain she wanted to marry Teddy. But she had also made the decision not to become sexually involved with anyone before marriage.

Her answer:

"Teddy, if you and I are right for each other, I can absolutely guarantee you it will fit."

I'd be some kind of crock out of the stone age to say that young sex is no good. It can be fascinating, exciting, a powerful pull body to body. But I still believe sex is for marriage, because, to say it again:

Great sex is not simply the coming together
of two bodies.
It is the total blending of two lives,
getting it all together.
And that, I believe, is the way God intended sex to be.

Often young people ask me, "When do you run out of sex?" ... "Is it true that it isn't any good after you're fifty?"

Have I got news for you!

Sex, when it's right, gets better and better. And for two people I know it never has been better than it is at sixty-three.

But your sex is your decision. It's yours to make beautiful, yours to misuse. So will you believe me enough to get away by yourself and do a deep think on this:

"My sex is a part of my total being. I do not choose to leave a little bit of me here, a little bit of me there. The more I cherish my total self now, the more I can bring to a marriageable love."

For the Sexuality Questionnaire see Appendix. This one is entitled "Your Sexual I.Q."

Money: Those big beautiful dollars. Will they be a magnet drawing us closer or a sinister wedge?

7

The Money Test

Over and over and over I hear the money questions.
They come in many combinations, and in this chapter
we will look at some of the most difficult. If any of
these ring warning bells in you, the time to listen is
before marriage.

Those big beautiful dollars can be the means of
drawing two people together or they can divide. They
can provide pain or pleasure, fussing or fun, the good
life or the ugly. And which they provide depends in
large part on how much a couple will confront their
basic attitudes and talk about them. Where are the
possible conflict areas? For an answer to that question
we will be taking a look at the trouble spots where
they're happening.

However, before you read further, turn to the
Money Questionnaire in the Appendix. Evaluate
your friend's attitude toward money and ask your
friend to evaluate yours. Then compare answers
and discuss.

NOT TIGHT, BUT TIGHT-LIPPED

Natalie:

"Shouldn't you expect to talk about finances when you're engaged? Abe absolutely refuses to discuss money. He's going into the clothing store with his father, and I guess he thinks the way his father does it is good enough for us. His father never tells his mother anything about their money. He just gives her an allowance to run the household. From the way they live, I know it must be a generous allowance, but I still don't think I would like it.

"I once had a chance to discuss this with Abe's aunt and she said all the women from their background expect it to be that way. Well, that may be O.K. for them, but I have been working for a long time and have been managing my own money. I don't like the way they do it. I think this could be bad. Is there anything I can do?"

Love, during the engagement, has a tendency to shelve potential problem areas. But Natalie is wise not to let this one be shelved. Her options are:

(a) to resign her own independence and live on an allowance;

(b) issue an edict: "Abe, you will either be open to discussion and compromise'';

or

(c) "the engagement is off."

THE RICH AND NOT SO RICH

Vic: "Millicent is from a very wealthy family. She isn't spoiled and you would really never know it. Sometimes though I think about how it would be to marry Millicent. Maybe this sounds old-fashioned, but I have always thought it would be nice to have a wife and family depending on me. Do you think the wife having all that much money would take something away? That is what I want to know."

Holly: "I'm engaged to this boy whose father is a millionaire and lately I've been noticing some things. Like he seems to be unhappy so much of the time. So what I've been thinking is, could this be because he doesn't really have any challenge? And could a marriage to someone like that be more difficult?"

Yes, it could. Money does strange things to people, and some of the strange things it does can affect a marriage forever.

I have known a few happy couples where one was "rich" and the other was not. So it can be done, but in asking how it was done, I come up with these blunt answers:

(1) a mousy woman;

(2) a man who didn't mind being kept;

(3) a high sense of humor on both sides;

(4) couples who loved each other with a mature love, mature enough to accept facts and adjust to them.

Vic's question, "What will her money do to *me*?" is a must for any combination of "the rich and not so rich."

Holly's question is equally sharp: "What will his money do to *him*?"

The old adage "constant dripping wears away the stone" applies. Sometimes if we fail to settle a problem before marriage, that problem gradually changes both of us until different people emerge.

Money, and our attitude toward it through the years, can work changes to our detriment or changes to our betterment. *Which will it be?*

DO WE WANT THE SAME THINGS?

"Do we agree on the meaning of success?" ...
"What are your goals? Mine?" ... "Do we want the
same things?"

These questions, and others like them, are too often
unasked. I know, because I see a steady parade of
these non-askers in my consultation room.

Leading the list is a hard-charger husband and his
lonesome wife. From a letter:

"I've decided to get a divorce, and I don't like it.
But I don't know what else to do. From the very beginning one of Stanley's goals has been to make a million dollars. Well, he's almost there and now would
you believe he wants another million?

"All our married life he has been saying, 'When we
make our first million, we'll travel, buy anything you
ever wanted, live it up.'

"But he didn't mean it, and I was a fool to believe
he ever did. Now I can see it's beginning to affect the
children, so I guess I don't have any other choice except to turn my back on what could have been so
fine."

I wonder how much these
two communicated prior to
their marriage. How much
did they discuss common
values? Did they even try to
reach an agreement between
his financial goals and her
feeling that other things were
more important?

Sometimes it is the wife who wants more, more, more, and the husband's drive doesn't match her ambition.

When Marv and Phyllis married, they didn't have much. But two people so much in love didn't need much. Unfortunately, they spent so much time looking dreamily at each other that they didn't look far enough into the future. Gradually, they began to part company inside. Phyllis wanted the best of everything. She wanted the best home, best car, best clothes; wanted to belong to the best clubs and circulate with the "best" people.

But there sat "good ol' Marv" in his comfortable rocker, smoking his pipe, taking it easy. The kids were well fed, they had clothes, shoes. They lived in a "homey" house; had a regular paycheck; their time payments weren't exorbitant; and they had lots of friends. So what could the matter be?

Nothing the matter, provided two people can live with it, but Phyllis can't live with it.

Same question:
Why didn't Marv and
Phyllis define "success"
before they married? Why
didn't they compare their
basic natures and come to
some agreement?

DOUBLE INCOME vs. SINGLE

Have you considered the question of double income versus single? Many working couples I know fail to ask, "When we start a family, what happens? Will she go back to work? If so, how soon? Does he believe that no matter what, a mother ought to be at home? Will she be totally content with total domesticity? Can we live on a single income?"

Marriageable love at its
best faces all possibilities, all
choices, all ramifications.

PENURIOUS

"I hate to say this but sometimes I think Edward is plain tight. You wouldn't believe the number of times I have to pay the bill when we eat out. He says he forgets to bring enough money with him. I wish I could believe it is that simple, but I think it is something else. I learned a new word in my English class this year and I think it describes Edward. The word is penurious and it means stingy. Can a man ever get over this?"

Yes, he can get over it, but
here are the two familiar
"if's" again:
  if he will admit he has a
problem;
  if he will go far enough
back to see what made him
penurious.

THE COMPULSIVE SPENDER

"Sylvia is always running up bills, and it seems like every time she gets paid she goes out and buys something else. Sometimes the things she buys don't even seem to make sense to me. You wouldn't believe the monthly payments she lets herself in for. Sylvia and I have so much going for us, but I ask myself: could I ever earn enough money to keep up with her?"

Keep asking. I know a couple where the wife is like this, but they get along well. She has agreed to let him set a limit beyond which she will not spend.

Then there are husbands who spend as if money is going out of style. One of our "spendy" friends turns his paycheck over to his wife and asks her to give him an allowance. For them it works.

We also know couples whose financial condition can only be described as chaotic; always broke; always in debt; bankrupt.

Incisive question for every couple: Are we financially solvent, not in dollars and cents, but in our attitudes?

INTEGRITY

In mathematics the "integer" is a number not divided into fractions. This is the basis of our word integrity. A person of integrity is whole, not divided. His beliefs and his performance are not in conflict. So what does this have to do with money?

One answer: "Mike is with an insurance company and he travels. He earns a good salary, and I do not think we would ever have any money problems, because I am a medical technician and have a fine income too. Then why am I writing you? I am worried about Mike's thinking. He brags about cheating on his expense account. This isn't like Mike. He is a very religious person and knows the difference between right and wrong. Yet when we discuss it, he says, 'Oh everybody does it.' This worries me."

Worries me too. I have known many men like Mike, and some women. There is a verse in the Song of Solomon which says, "Take me the foxes, the little foxes which spoil the vines." Behind this passage is an interesting explanation. The big foxes were no problem. They couldn't get through small holes. But the little foxes could slip into a vineyard and do big damage almost before anyone knew they were there.

Important question: With our individual tendencies and our combination of tendencies, what little foxes could spoil the vines?

THE GIVER AND THE NONGIVER

Seth is a Mormon. Raised in a devout Mormon home, trained in a long line of tithers, he's a big giver. His family has always given ten percent of their income to the church. With all his soul Seth believes in this practice, and he practices what he believes.

Joyce grew up in a home where religion was "take it or leave it." Her family was not much concerned with the needs of others. She doesn't understand that word "mission" which she hears so much from Seth.

Can any couple raised in such totally different families come to some agreement they can live with?

Answer: Yes. We know, because we did it in our marriage. Early in our relationship Martha and I adopted this plan:

"Give ten percent.
Save ten percent.
Spend the rest with
thanksgiving and
praise."

For us it has been simply super.

Have you worked out a common philosophy of saving, giving, spending?

TWO CHECKING ACCOUNTS

Herly and Agnes have separate checking accounts. They come from backgrounds almost identical at this point . . . they were taught to rely on themselves! Circumstances made it necessary for them to manage on their own. Obviously, these two "do-your-own-thing" people might have been headed for a collision. He took it for granted he'd keep the books. She took it for granted this was one thing any efficient wife would do.

Big question: Could these two autonomous personalities work out a compromise?

Big answer: Every month when the pay check comes, they divide it down the middle, half for each.

When they decided to experiment with this, they split the living costs. He would take A, B, C. She would pay X, Y, Z. But in addition to their expenses, they would each have their own checking accounts (in different banks); they would each have some for saving; they would each have some miscellaneous pocket money.

And here's the bottom line: Herly and Agnes have had their separate accounts for thirty-eight years.

Never do at our house. "Don't bother me with anything more than a general report. I have important things to do. You keep the books, Martha."

(Interesting side note: Herly and Agnes don't agree on grocery stores either. So? So they take turns buying the family groceries at their own favorite store.)

Sounds of the freedom bell again. Liberty. Independence. "You do it your way. I do it mine!"

Money is one place where a couple can blend each to his own and both together.

Super agreement:
   We will have fun with our money.
   We will give.

We will save.

And above all we will stay in control of our dollars and cents.

They will never, absolutely never, control us!

Distance: looking forward; evaluating the future; seeing into the years ahead.

8

The Distance Test

Dear Dr. Shedd:

I read one time that a boy should take a look at his girl's mother, because maybe she is going to look like that someday. Well, Connie doesn't look like her mother now, except in the face. Connie has a good figure, and I get turned on by almost everything about her. She is so smart, very religious, but a lot of fun.

Maybe I shouldn't say it, but you should see her mother. She looks like the back end of a Mack truck. Do you think Connie will look like that after a while?

I don't think I could take it to be married to Connie if she looked like her mother. Of course, I know it would still be Connie underneath, but can you imagine? What do you think?

Steve

I like this letter and the way Steve is thinking ahead. Twenty years from now when he looks at her across the breakfast table, will he still like what he sees?

And will she?

Today's young set amazes me and this is one reason —they are not only willing, but eager, to look ahead. We grew up in a generation where we waited for love to "happen" and when it "happened," we went to the altar without much prethink. But now many won't settle for that. Whether it is by mail, one-on-one consultation, group encounter, I hear a constant refrain which sounds like, "Hand us the binoculars."

To this point we have been concentrating on the majors:

Transparency
Liberty
Unselfishness
Mercy
Apology
Sexuality
Money

In our Distance test we focus on items miscellaneous. These are possible problem areas which surface often enough to merit consideration.

1. HOME AND FAMILY

ATTITUDE TOWARD PARENTS

Steve is checking size. Jill is concerned with something else.

"There is one thing I worry about Eric. It seems as if he doesn't like his parents enough. And sometimes I even wonder if he hates them. I have always liked my dad and mom. Well, not always, but most of the time. Yet Eric keeps telling me he doesn't think my folks are so great either. And I get the feeling he doesn't want me to like them. It makes me wonder. What do you think?"

Before you read my answer, you work out your own answer. Or better still you and your friend discuss it. What do the two of you think?

> I think—Jill is wise to be wondering. People like Eric are often burning with unsettled hostility. Crucial question: Will he face the fact that *he* might be at fault somewhere? Would he be willing to talk to a counselor to help him sort this out? Unless he agrees to look in the mirror, whoever marries Eric may be in for big trouble. The reason? Old hostility brought into marriage is often transferred from former targets to the mate.

BEHAVIOR OF PARENTS

Here's another smart girl checking. She writes; "Jimmy is so sweet and most of the time he's very nice to me. But when I'm at his house for dinner, I can hardly stand the way Jimmy's father talks to Jimmy's mother. Some of the things he says to her would just kill me. Do you think Jimmy would ever be like that?"

In your opinion, would he?

I think—Yes, Jimmy might
be like that. The imprints
on our minds are often
sound tracked early. Then
again he might not. And
one reason he might not is
that some people are sharp
enough to pick out
negatives in their history
and turn in the opposite
direction. Another
important question: What
does *Jimmy* think about his
father's treatment of his
mother?

MARITAL HISTORY

Mark:
   "My aunt says you should only marry someone from a
happy home, because you would have a better chance for a
happy marriage. Well, my girl's parents are divorced. It
really broke her up, and I understand. But do you think we
could make it?"

   Is Marks' aunt right?
   And what if she is?
   How much should we narrow our field?
   If we were to take all the people from
broken homes and scratch them from our list
of possibilities that wouldn't be fair, would
it?

Straight from Annie,
another answer; this one
flashing back to the fact that
some people take an opposite
turn:
   "Because my parents were
divorced when I was eleven,
I decided that if I ever got
married, I'd be such a great
wife, my husband would
never want to leave me."

For musing: "Same fire hardens the egg
            and melts the butter."

THE HOUSE THEY LIVE IN

Neal:
   "When I go to Mariann's house, I get very nervous. You
should see it. You can hardly sit down without taking some
magazines or old newspapers out of the chairs, or a fly
swatter, or some dirty socks. Then on the end table there
might be empty coffee cups and ashtrays which are full, and
a bunch of Coke bottles and maybe half of an old sandwich.
   "Well, I come from a neat home and I like it that way.
What I am wondering is, would a girl raised in this kind of
house get so used to it she wouldn't even see how things
are?"

                  Would she?
        Checking each other's home has to be
        good. Order? Cleanliness? And how about
        the cooking?
             One young clown said (this time he was

really serious): "I can hardly stand to eat at her house. I kid you not, they put cheese dressing on everything. First time, I thought, Oh well. But then they did it again. Holy cow! Can you imagine? Cheese dressing on *everything*?"

Keep trying to imagine! A couple married fifty years may spend 18,250 days under the same roof and eat 54,750 meals together. (Cheese dressing on everything?)

Since habits are hard to break, this is another important question:

Even if changes are made at the outset, how long will they last? Most of us have a way of reverting to former patterns.

2. WORK HABITS

Susan is in graduate school, engaged to Jerry. But now it has happened again. Jerry has quit his job. Fourth job he's quit in three years since he graduated. This time he says the boss was impossible. On job number one he didn't like the people he was working with. Then quotas were too high; nobody could make that many sales in one month. So now comes the sneaky question:

Is Jerry a floater?

Susan:

"Is something the matter with Jerry instead of with his jobs? Would he be unhappy wherever he worked? I'm not used to all these changes. I graduated from high school in the same town where I was born. My father has been in business there for thirty years. I guess it could be me."

> Important questions for any couple in almost any problem area:
> Are we willing to quit talking excuses and deal with reasons?
> If Susan were asking you, what would you advise her?
> In your relationship, can you come up with a definition of stability which makes sense for both of you?

3. SUBTLE SHADINGS OF PERSONALITY

We have been looking at some of the easy check places. But in addition to visible matters, each of us has beneath the surface subtle shadings of attitude and disposition which should also be considered.

Two examples:

"WHY RISK IT?" vs. "LET'S TRY IT."

Jason and Melissa are college seniors. They have gone together two years and he is beginning to ask himself if they could make it.

"My problem is something I hardly ever see mentioned and Melissa doesn't think it's much of a problem, but I wonder if you think it is serious.

"Melissa was raised by parents who were always telling her, 'Be careful' ... 'You might get sick' ... 'What if you get hurt?'

"I know they must have said this a lot when she was growing up, because even now, when she is a college senior, they still do it.

"Me? I was raised to really give it fits. You know, live, enjoy. My folks taught me not to be stupid, but they sure taught me not to hang back.

"Melissa questions almost everything I do. Like this weekend I am going mountain climbing with two of my fraternity brothers. It really isn't much of a mountain, but you'd think it was the Matterhorn the way she keeps at me. Is there any way I can get Melissa to change, and if she won't, do you think we would make it?"

Sorry, Jason, I can't be optimistic about ever changing Melissa into the "high adventure" type. So you're right to be concerned. You might be miserable; plus those whose nature is "Let's sit by the fire" find it frustrating to sit by the fire alone, and they worry about their mate out in the dangerous world having fun.

You are faced with the question: "Is there enough good in our relationship to make up for the gap between her caution and my derring-do?"

I can't make this decision

for you. But I can tell you (since I am very much your type), it is simply great to live with a woman who is unafraid of life, unafraid of the world, unafraid of the new.

Before you read on, turn to the Appendix, and work the Distance Questionnaire.

THE NEED FOR COMPANIONSHIP

Cherie has completed her second year at a southern university. She and Kevin are very much in love. He's the big man on campus, expects to make All-American this year.

Problem? Kevin spends almost all his time with football. He studies the football playbook, practices, goes out with his teammates, watches the games on television, hopes someday to play with the pros.

Meanwhile back in her dormitory room, Cherie is doing some serious thinking.

"I guess I'm the kind who has to spend hours, not minutes, with the person I love. I know Kevin loves me his way, but a few minutes over a Coke now and then, or a couple of dates each week are simply not enough. We have already decided we would be married this summer. But now I'm not so sure.

"Is it true, like Kevin says, that when you get married you naturally spend more time together? I know that's right to a certain extent, but what if Kevin never needed to be with me like I need to be with him? So my big question is, with my being the way I am and

Kevin the way he is, should I marry him?"
Should she?
How do you evaluate their possibilities?

This is what I call high-risk engagement. Grade it "F."
The land is full enough of lonesome wives without Cherie adding her name to the list.
Cherie may have come from a home where people were constantly drawing close. Or maybe they didn't, and that could be why she needs more time than Kevin is giving her. Family backgrounds do matter here. But so do individual differences. Our Creator made all of us with variant degrees of interdependency and self-containment.
On a thermometer measuring the need for companionship, where would you place yourself?
Your friend?
If seventy is the healthy temperature, are you both above seventy? Below? Or is there so much spread you should do a retake?

One of the smoothest organizations I know in big business has a top executive with this unusual title: "Vice-President of Forward Planning." His job is to take all the different things going on in the company, evaluate them, and see what effect they might have down the road.

Maybe one of the reasons they are such a smooth organization is their constant scanning of tomorrow.

Let's now have a meeting, just the two of us, and elect each other Vice-President of Forward Planning.

Fun: Laughter, levity,
merriment and mirth?
Yes, but more
than these the ability
to enjoy people; to enjoy
the world; and
to feel together
"the birds are singing
just for us."

9

The Fun Test

Dear Dr. Shedd:

I have this very serious problem, which I have never talked to anyone about, but I think it is time for me to face it because I am so emotionally involved. I need help.

Jonathan and I have gone together four years, and I am very much in love with him. But something is wrong. First I want to tell you all the good things about him. He is kind to me and thoughtful. He is so smart and I know he will be an excellent provider, because that is the type of person he is. He is handsome and I am proud to be seen with him. My folks like him too. Also I am the star of our women's basketball team, and although he is not athletic, he is proud of me.

So you ask, what can be wrong? I will tell you. It is that he isn't any fun. By fun I mean being with people, getting into their heads, laughing, talking with people, enjoying them. By fun I also mean doing things on the spur of the moment, suddenly changing your plans, going places you hadn't thought of, doing different things.

Well, Jonathan isn't really all that interested in people except me. I honestly think if I were the only person on earth besides him, he would be happy. When we go to a party, I move around while he just sits there.

Then when it comes to doing things on the spur of the moment, do you think Jonathan would ever change his mind? Never. He plans everything and I do mean everything. Every date, every weekend, every semester, everything he does, he plans and never changes. If I suggest anything different or if anything forces him to vary his plans, he gets terribly upset.

So my question is do you think fun is all that important if you have someone who offers everything except fun? Should I go ahead and marry him?

Love,
Gail

From me, a loud "NO!" Don't marry him. In marriageable love, fun is a major "major."

I like the fact that Gail has defined fun for her. Good thinking. Many people, when they hear the word "fun" associate laughter, humor, hilarity and a gay time. Nothing the matter with these either, but fun in its broader concept includes many other things. And one thing it doesn't include for some of us is a "blueprint" life.

A DEFINITION OF FUN

Fun is anything a couple does
   which they both enjoy
   which contributes to their well being,

           physically
             mentally
               spiritually
which draws them closer together
which gives them an appreciation of each other's
interests
which develops their talents and abilities
which makes life more interesting
which creates enthusiasm
    provides zest
        adds touches of excitement
which takes them new places
which gives purpose to their life together.

What would the two of you add to this definition?

THE ENDLESS VARIETIES OF FUN

Comes now a list of fun things we have seen couples
do. They have collected:

art   coins   bottles   matchbook covers   china   stamps
spoons   pewter   coffee mugs   beer mugs   shaving mugs
mustache cups   stoneware   glassware   copperware
clocks   trunks   two-dollar bills   commemorative plates
butter molds   ice-cream freezers   hand-made quilts   and
would you believe old-fashioned "potty" jars?

You name it, some couple somewhere is having fun
collecting it.

We know couples who are into:
photography . fishing   scrimshaw   square dance
downhill skiing   cross country skiing   water skiing

painting   antique cars   jogging   stained glass   old films
golf   theater   bicycling   pottery   sculpting   snorkeling
poetry   deep sea diving   guitar   Angora cats   Abyssian
cats   Calico cats   Himalayan cats   Persian cats
Siamese cats   alley cats   parakeets   canaries   exotic fish
quarter horses   Arabians   thoroughbreds   Welsh ponies
Shetland ponies   painted ponies   Nubian goats
Charolais cattle   chinchillas
sailing   canoeing   motorboating   lapidaria   macrame
gemology   vegetable gardening   flower gardening
organic gardening   building zithers   building harps
building clocks   astronomy   astrology   archeology
country music   rock music   sacred music   symphony
opera   jazz

And we have other friends who have done other
things interesting to them but so uninteresting to us we
have forgotten what they were.

"NOBODY HAS HAD MORE FUN THAN WE'VE HAD"

I would wish for you that after almost forty years
together, you could say, "Nobody has had more fun
than we've had." Then I would also wish that you
could add, "No couple on earth is having more fun
than we're having now."

Sure, we've had our low moments. Very low.
We've had days when we didn't enjoy each other,
times when we didn't even like each other. We've had
periods of fussing, drawing apart, closing doors,
building walls.

But when we ask: What has kept us moving in the

110

right direction, growing closer? One answer has to be, "the fun we've had."

Like?

Exercise. For a time we were into jogging. Then we golfed. Next we bowled. Now it's tennis.

We've also been big on *animals*. One time in our early history we raised dogs; bred them; showed them; made some interesting shaggy friends; some of whom looked exactly like their dogs. Then we went into rabbits. Fur rabbits. We traveled to rabbit shows; studied rabbit literature; and from all our rabbit doings we learned more than anyone ever needed to know about rabbits. We've also raised Manx cats, the cats without tails, fascinating.

Collecting? Things too numerous to mention we've collected. But the collection which has meant most is our Heads of Christ collection. Through the years we have visited artists; made slides; given lectures; used our collection for counseling; and grown somehow with each addition.

THE LASTING HOBBIES

Some hobbies finally conclude themselves. Others for us seem to mean more with every passing year.

Woodworking: building furniture, shopping for old treasures, rebuilding, restoring, refinishing.

The beach: Driftwood. Shells. The bird scenario. Great white birds with long neck, yellow bill, black feet. Huge gray birds gliding by like giant cargo carriers. Tiny birds hopping on one foot.

The tides, coming and going with punctilious regularity. Changing color of the marshes, sunset over the water, full moon, sunrise.

Combining their awe, all these bring us to a pure reverence in our togetherness.

I hope you like nature together because if you do, the world and everything in it can be yours to enjoy with each other.

TWO TRAPS FOR CHECKING

Trap 1. Some lovers we know, some husbands and wives, spend so much time with other people, they have too little time with each other. Group get-to-gethers are fun. So are family reunions, dinner with friends, parties. Nothing the matter with social gatherings. We need them, and if we're the kind of people we ought to be, they need us.

But this stuff is like dope, easy to get on and hard to get off. We can become so hooked on "otherness" our "togetherness" gets away.

Same thing when the children come. Fun with the family is an absolute must. Children who can look back to their home with positive recall are more likely to be stable adults. But here too the wise couple will reserve time for themselves, time to be alone, time to develop their own fun.

Trap 2. In any way, does your friend's fun border on an obsession?

"Larry is a super tennis player. I think he would rather play tennis than eat. And sometimes I know he'd rather play tennis than be with me."

"She's an artist and I honestly think her ability to enjoy anything other than art will always be limited."

112

"He's a fisherman, all fisherman, except now and then he goes hunting."

"Lucy is a concert pianist. She's got a lot going for her when she does get away from her piano, but we recently had this big fight and I told her, I don't think you should marry anyone Lucy, because you are already married to your piano."

Hear the moaning and groaning, from wives mostly, but now and then a husband whose marriage is missing this single ingredient: Fun with *the* one they'd like to have fun with.

And the sadness here is not of immediate moment only. Some of the saddest sadness comes from looking back. Is there anything sadder than the dawning realization, "We could have had so much fun together if only we had taken more time to have fun."

What kind of people will we be on our fiftieth anniversary?

Barney and his Martha are seventy-two. They have been married almost fifty years. They've had many hobbies, kept their minds alert, reading, studying, traveling.

Now they have taken up shrimping. If you could see them on the beach, you'd like what you see. There is Barney in his wet suit far out in the water, and Martha near shore holding her end of the net. Fun!

Ask it again: When we reach our fiftieth anniversary, will we be having fun?

For the Fun Questionnaire, see Appendix.

Holiness: awe, reverence, wonder, and all good things which come from tuning in to the Divine.

The Holiness Test

Dear Dr. Shedd:

I think real love is like it is between Billie Jean and me. What I mean is we are both better people when we are together than when we are alone.

Sometimes when we are parked on the hill that overlooks our town, or if we are walking together, or just sitting still beside each other, we get this feeling like there is Someone there with us. You know, not two of us, but three.

I guess this is what they mean when they use the word, "Holy." Anyhow that is what it is like to us, and we both think it is the most beautiful thing that ever happened.

                                        Randy

I think so too, and if I could give every one of my single friends a single gift it would be this:

That they might find a person with whom they could one day say: "Our duet at its best is a Trinity."

If you review these tests and ponder the various

people you know, you may say, "Impossible. I could never find anyone who meets all these requirements." True. But nobody has to be that wonderful to marry you. Why? Because you're not that wonderful now either. In the original maybe, but now?

Only a super egotist would say, "I've got it all together. I have arrived." This kind of self-perfection isn't the answer and we know it.

So what is the answer? The answer is that we are not required to be perfect. The God who made us in His image didn't go off and leave us. Deep in our hearts He still lives and if we turn Him loose to do His thing, miracles can happen now and in the future.

He can help us achieve the total honesty needed for total transparency.

Because He is the God of freedom, He sets us free to allow our mate to be free.

He provides mercy when our mind is set on revenge.

To our weak little trickles of humility He pours the floods of His Grace, making it possible for us to say, "I'm sorry" and "I forgive."

He can become our source of good times, joy, fun.

So how do we activate the Spirit in us? How do we turn the Lord loose to achieve His dream for our lives?

Our land is full of yogis and swamis with and without turban, crying, "Lo here, lo there." So who really does have the answer? I think everybody has a piece of the answer.

There is a lovely legend about creation day. When God had finished his work, He assigned responsibilities. For carrying the pearl of truth to earth He chose a very small boy. That would be like God, but He really shouldn't have done it. Little one tripped on a cloud and dropped the pearl, so when it fell to earth it broke into a million pieces.

Is that why the voices cry, "See here it is! I found it! This is truth."

Yes, it's truth, a fragment. But the God of all truth has some truth reserved especially for you; and in addition He has some reserved for you and your loved one together. Sure, there are verities which come under the heading "Truth for all God's children." Yet a part of His genius is that He speaks individually to individuals. And some of us have learned from experience that He has a very special way of speaking to two individuals tuning in together to His love.

THE QUIET TIME

My wife and I were living in a big city. All kinds of opportunities to experiment, to test this truth and that. There was a veritable smorgasbord of so-called spiritual food. And behind the counter pushy people saying, "You must have some of mine." . . . "Don't pass this by." . . . "What we have here is guaranteed to satisfy."

So we tasted this, tasted that, and nothing tasted quite right for us. Finally we decided there was only one thing left. We would work out our own method of getting us together with the Lord.

The basis for our oneness from that day on has been our daily quiet time. It is a time of reading together, reading alone, a time for thinking, meditating, sharing our thoughts.

It is also a time for prayer. But right here with most couples, the whole thing comes to a screeching halt. To be completely open with the Lord and one other person can be frightening. "What will he think of what I'm saying to God?" "Will she understand the things I ask for?"

That's how we felt, and because we felt that way, we decided on silent prayer. Before we prayed silently together, we would discuss, we would share from the deep places and then we would pray. But we soon learned this too: Some feelings can not be expressed in words. So we would hold hands and in the stillness open our hearts together.

If this sounds right for you, here are some suggestions:

Choose a favorite spot. Through the years our rocking love seat has become the most beautiful chapel anywhere on earth for us. Of course we pray in other places—in the car, walking the beach, watching the sunset, anywhere. Still for us the regular place for regular prayer is a good thing.

Set up a goal. Hurry, hurry, hurry. Rush, rush, rush. Get a move on. Zip, zam, zowie do we live. So this is a fact: the quiet time better be scheduled. It's easy to fall into the trap of believing that tomorrow, next week, six months from now we will have big chunks of time for developing our oneness.

But that's not true. We have as much time today as we will have tomorrow. So what can we do to be in control of our time and not vice versa?

The surest answer we found was this understanding: The more we had to do, the more we needed our quiet time. When we began to see it that way, we committed ourselves to practice the Quiet time daily, regularly. At first we set up a goal of doing it more often than we didn't, or fifty-one percent of the time. Then we built from there until it has become almost a must for us. And through it all, as we drew closer to God, we drew closer to each other. Closer in soul. Closer in mind. Closer in body.

Of course, we have grown to the place where we can pray aloud now. You wouldn't believe our vocal prayer. Conversing, interrupting, arguing, laughing, melding.

Yet even today we revert to silent prayer, because sometimes there are things best shared in silence.

Will our method work for you? It doesn't matter. Truth is, the "How to pray" question is not as important as "Do we pray?" If you do, regularly, you will be led to ways of prayer especially right for you. And when you find them, you have found the secret to marriageable love, before marriage, after marriage, and forever.

"Have a good day" ... "a good evening" ... "Have a good weekend" ... "a good trip" ... "Have a good semester." These happy little sayings are a big improvement over "So long" ... "Take it easy" ... "Now you be good."

Recently I came on what I think is the ultimate of the "have a good" series. The expansive soul who thought this one up didn't miss one single thing:

121

"Have A Good Forever!"

I like that. I want that. I want that for me, for the person I love most; for you, and the person you love.

Could it be that what we achieve in human harmony here does make a difference hereafter? No question in my mind. I have always believed that.

So this is my wish for you:

That you and the person you marry

may have touches of heaven on earth.

But even more I wish for you

that you may:

HAVE A GOOD FOREVER!

Appendix
Questionnaires

The questionnaires which follow are in duplicate so that you and your friend may work them independently. You may be tempted to think, "With our closeness, we can do these together." Closeness is a real plus, but even the best relationships need frequent checking. If you each work the questionnaire alone, you will have a clearer picture of your potential. Some questions are for judging yourself. Others are for evaluating your friend. The real value of these questionnaires comes when you compare answers and discuss.

The Transparency Questionnaire

1. I come from a family where people were more open to each other than closed. Yes____ No____

2. On a scale of 1 to 10 (10 being perfect) I rate my honesty with other people. ____
   My honesty with myself. ____

3. When I'm angry I tend to submerge my feelings. Yes____ No____

4. When I am moody, I am willing to accept help in understanding my gloom. Yes____ No____
   I resent people asking me why I am down. Yes____ No____
   I tend to clam up. Yes____ No____

5. I can see the humorous side of me when someone points it out and usually I can even laugh at myself. Yes____ No____

6. I would be willing to read material which would help us to know each other better. Yes____ No____

7. On the scale of 1 to 10 I rate our overall transparency now: ____
   I rate our wish to know each other's feelings: ____
   I rate the growth in honesty between us: ____

The Liberty Questionnaire

On a scale of 1 to 10 rate your marriage potential.

1. In general respect for the other person's rights and for individual differences, I rate my friend: ____

2. With some people I feel pressure to agree. With others I can relax and express my feelings. Between us I think my friend and I rate: ____

3. There are things I am not ready to share yet, but would like to sometime. Yes____ No____

4. Some people are too pushy when it comes to another person's thoughts. Others have a genuine respect for privacy. Here I grade my friend: ____

5. When we are together I can even talk about some of my fantasies without fear of being put down. Because this kind of relationship takes time, I rate our possibilities here: ____

6. Freedom to talk isn't the only freedom. Freedom to "do" is also important. My friend is good about letting me participate in certain activities by myself. Yes____ No____

My friend also encourages me to enjoy friends of my own. Yes____ No____

The Unselfishness Questionnaire

1. The Bible says, "They that would have friends must show themselves friendly." Most of the time friendly people are not selfish people. They have the ability to get out of the way enough to concentrate on others. Does your friend have many friends? Yes____ No____

2. Few of us enjoy going out of our way to please the selfish. Is your friend the kind of person for whom other people like to do things? Yes____ No____

3. When you are planning something together, does your friend:

A. Ask you what you think first? ____
B. Tell you, "Here's what I think" and expect you to agree? ____
C. Pout if you get your way? ____

4. Are the words "thank you" heard often enough in your relationship? Genuine gratitude is another characteristic of the unselfish. On the grading scale 1 to 10 how do you grade your friend as a "thanker"? ____

5. How long has it been since your friend surprised you with some special little extra which seemed to say, "I think you're extra special?" ____

6. Some people are selfish because they were "spoiled" as children. They were given everything they wanted, almost as soon as they wanted it. Others had less than those around them and as a result, they are out to get their share.

Some home backgrounds were just right. In any way do you consider your friend "damaged" by too much or too little? Yes___No___Were you? Yes___No___ Discuss together.

7. If the two of you had a job to do together and it was not your favorite thing, but it had to be done, would you expect:

A. You would end up doing more than your share. ___
B. Your friend would really pitch in. ___
C. You would divide it equally. ___

8. Which collection of words do you hear most often in your relationship?

"I" "Me" "My" "Mine" and the sounds of self-centered thinking. ___
"You" "Yours" "We" "Us" Our" "Ours" and the indicators of genuine "otherness" ___

The Mercy-Apology Questionnaire

1. Do you sometimes feel your friend is overcritical of others? Yes___ No___
And is your friend overcritical of you? Yes___ No___

2. Does your friend tend to gossip? Yes___ No___

3. Do you consider your friend generally positive about other people? Yes___ No___

4. When you tell your friend, "You're wrong," is the reaction likely to be (check one or more):
   defensive ___
   "I'm sorry" ___
   silent ___
   argumentative ___
   "I'll try to do better" ___
   angry ___
   grateful ___
   don't care ___

5. How long does it usually take your friend to apologize? ___

6. Does you friend tend to bring up past negatives in your relationship? Yes___ No___

7. Have you and your friend had an agreement on what to tell? How much to tell? Yes___ No___

Your Sexual IQ Test

1

Were you well trained early about sex? Yes____ No____

Did your parents give you adequate information as you needed it? Yes____ No____

On the scale of 1 to 10 (10 for perfect) grade your early sex education. ____

2

Do you know the correct words for the sex organs; for the different kinds of sexual activity? Yes____ No____

Do you know the meanings of the dirty words? Yes____ No____

How would you grade your sex vocabulary? (1 to 10) ____

3

Do you tend too much toward dirty stories, sexy jokes, shady humor? Yes____ No____

Are you overly interested in pornography, skin flicks, nude pictures, sex books? Yes____ No____

Put your sex attitudes up against the word "clean" and grade yourself 1 to 10. ____

4

Can you take a stand for what you think is right and make it stick? Yes____ No____

Would you let someone talk you into doing something you don't believe in? Yes____ No____

Grade yourself on your ability to do your own thing. (1 to 10) ____

5

Do you really have a feeling for the other person's feelings? Yes____ No____

Do you tend to pressure others too much to get your own way? Yes____ No____

Grade your overall respect for the beliefs, the morals, the standards of other people. (1 to 10) ____

6

Do you really care what your parents think? Yes____ No____

Would you ever do anything drastic to spite them, punish them, get even? Yes____ No____

How do you grade the climate between you and your parents? (1 to 10) ____

7

Are you acquainted with the laws of God (about sex) and have you decided what He expects of you personally? Yes____ No____

Do you think of God primarily as a punisher of evil? Yes____ No____

Or as a good friend who really cares about you? Yes____ No____

Grade your sense of responsibility to God (1 to 10) ____

8

Do you feel that you are normal in every way sexually? Yes____ No____

Do you look forward to building a happy sex life with the right person at the right time? Yes____ No____

For natural urges, self-control, healthy anticipation grade yourself (1 to 10) ____

The Money Questionnaire

Select the words which best describe your friend's attitude toward money:

careful _____
controlled _____
easy spender _____
happy-go-lucky _____
generous _____
careless _____
penurious _____
greedy _____
saving _____
selfish _____
extravagant _____
poor manager _____
stingy _____
too ambitious _____

Distance Questionnaire

Check the words and phrases which best fit your friend.
    Why risk it? _____
    Let's try it _____
    Sure, we can make it _____
    You might get hurt _____
    When in doubt, don't _____
    When in doubt, do _____
        overprotective _____
        daring _____
        adventuresome _____
        hesitant _____
        timid _____
        bold _____
        cautious _____
        curious _____

Listed here is a group of quotations from my Miscellany file. These are from people asking how their particular doubts, their wonderings might affect their future marriage. Check those you think need discussing between you.

_____ "Sometimes Andy drinks too much. He says when we are married, he'll cut down. Do you think he will?"

_____ "Melanie's folks don't like me, especially her mother. Is it all that important for a girl's parents to like the man she is going to marry?"

_____ "My boy friend is O.K. with me when we're alone, but when any of his friends are around, he acts like he didn't even know me. What do you think is the matter?"

_____ "The one thing we wonder about is the way we fight all the time. My sister says not to worry, because she and her husband fight a lot and they're still together. But I'm not so sure. Wouldn't this get tiresome?"

_____ "I'm studying for my Master's in foreign languages. The man I'm engaged to didn't finish high school. I have to admit that when someone asks me where he went to college, I am somewhat embarrassed. How much priority should a couple give to common educational levels?"

_____ "Barbie has migraine headaches. Sometimes this worries me, because when I attended one of their family reunions it seemed all the women did was talk about how bad they felt. Should I tell Barbie?"

_____ "I never thought this would happen, but I think I am falling in love with Milton. He is in the Air Corps, which creates a problem. I was brought up in a pacifist home where the military was always put down. I have honestly tried to get over this, but it is very hard for me. Milton is wild about flying and he plans to stay in for a career. Neither one of us knows what to do. Can you help us?"

_____ "I am going with a man thirteen years older. My mother says that is too much difference, because he will be an old man when I am still young. She says she has seen it happen too often and I will be sorry if I marry him. Is that right?"

(Read the next two together).

_____ "My fiancee says she does not want to have children. Because the world is so mixed up, she says it wouldn't be fair to bring children into it. But my family has meant a lot to me and I have looked forward to having a family of my

134

own."

That statement comes from the male side. Now here is another, more familiar:

 "Craig is number one in our class, a real brain, but here is our problem. He says he never wants children and I know what he is thinking. He is afraid children would get in the way and take too much time. The truth is children are one of the big things with me, including other people's children. But mostly having children of my own. Do you think I should marry him and hope he will get over it?"

_____ "The man I am going with is more of a gentleman than anyone I've ever known. But there is one thing that bothers me. He is twenty-seven years old and still lives with his mother. In almost everything he does, it is like he checks with her. We have discussed marriage some, and if it gets more serious, do you feel I have anything to worry about?"

_____ "In our family my father was definitely head of the house and we all knew it and liked it. Even my mother liked it. But with Marshall and me, it's almost the exact opposite. It seems as if he leaves everything up to me. I don't mind sharing responsibility, but do you think it could ever work for a woman to take complete charge of everything?"

135

The Fun Questionnaire

TIME

1. I think my friend spends too much time on _____ and as I see it, this could develop into a problem between us. Yes____ No____

2. I believe there is a possibility we spend too much time with other people. Yes____ No____

  Not enough time. Yes____ No____

  About right. Yes____ No____

3. Here are some things we have never tried which I think might be fun for both of us: _____,

_____, _____.

FUN AND YOUR BASIC ATTITUDES

Are they right, those who say that all the world can be divided into two groups, Necrophiles and Biophiles? Necrophiles are the down-beat people. These are the lovers of doom, the pessimistic. Their thoughts turn to the dark and "Necro," meaning death, puts them on the side of, "Oh, isn't it awful?"

Biophiles move to the light. They are up with people, up with life, up with what's about to happen, expecting a miracle, optimistic.

Although it may be oversimplifying to divide the world and everyone in it by two categories, if you had to limit your choice to these two definitions, how would you rate your friend? Necrophile ____ Biophile ____

How do you rate yourself? Necrophile ____ Biophile ____

HUMOR

One indicator of people's fun philosophy is the humor they find attractive. Some get their jollies putting other people down, embarrassing others, ridiculing. These can be tough people to live with over the years.

Others include a shady touch in their fun. They get their laughs from the banal; the bawdy, the sometimes vulgar. West Point Cadets have a prayer: "Lord, if I can't be funny and clean, help me to only be clean."

Using the scale one to ten
For kindness in humor I rate my friend ___
My rating ___
Against the prayer of the West Point cadets, I rate my friend's humor ___
Mine ___

THEOLOGY

Theology is a combination of the two words, "Theos" and "logos," meaning thoughts of God. Our theology can make a major difference in our ability to have fun.

Which of these words do you most often associate with God?

joy ___
light ___
gladness ___
likeable ___
friend ___
severe ___
judgment ___
stern ___
strict ___
authoritarian ___

Questions with Many Answers: What Do You Say?

When I was in college we had a professor of philosophy who would tease us with the test question: "Define the universe and give three examples."

Some questions coming my way are like that. There is no pat answer. Many of these are better discussed than jammed into a single letter or answered in a short time.

Listed here are questions in this category. Some can be answered several ways. This is a questionnaire where I hope you and your friend may make mecca to your favorite talking place and bend each other's ear.

Do you think God has one person in the whole world who is right for me?

Is there such a thing as love at first sight?

Is it possible to be in love with two people at the same time?

What do you think about black-white marriage?

What is the best age for marriage?

Is computer dating ever a good thing?

If I don't want to go with someone anymore, how can I tell them?

Isn't it true a man and woman can communicate without words?

If prayer draws two people closer in every way, is it wise to pray together when you know you can't get married for a while?

Do you think it is possible that you might quit growing in a relationship if you are having sex?

After you are married, how long should you wait to have children?

Should a woman work even if the couple has children?

Does it ever work for the man to stay home, do the housework, raise the children, while the wife earns the living?

If I am religious and my fiance is an agnostic, how could we have a good marriage?

My church says I should not marry, because I have been divorced. But I am in love. Should I do it anyway?

And now for the big one—
    What does it really mean to say:
        Marriage is not so much
        finding the right person
        As it is being the right person.

The Transparency Questionnaire

1. I come from a family where people were more open to each other than closed. Yes____ No____

2. On a scale of 1 to 10 (10 being perfect) I rate my honesty with other people. ____
   My honesty with myself. ____

3. When I'm angry I tend to submerge my feelings. Yes____ No____

4. When I am moody, I am willing to accept help in understanding my gloom. Yes____ No____
   I resent people asking me why I am down. Yes____ No____
   I tend to clam up. Yes____ No____

5. I can see the humorous side of me when someone points it out and usually I can even laugh at myself. Yes____ No____

6. I would be willing to read material which would help us to know each other better. Yes____ No____

7. On the scale of 1 to 10 I rate our overall transparency now: ____
   I rate our wish to know each other's feelings: ____
   I rate the growth in honesty between us: ____

The Liberty Questionnaire

On a scale of 1 to 10 rate your marriage potential.

1. In general respect for the other person's rights and for individual differences, I rate my friend: _____

2. With some people I feel pressure to agree. With others I can relax and express my feelings. Between us I think my friend and I rate: _____

3. There are things I am not ready to share yet, but would like to sometime. Yes_____ No_____

4. Some people are too pushy when it comes to another person's thoughts. Others have a genuine respect for privacy. Here I grade my friend: _____

5. When we are together I can even talk about some of my fantasies without fear of being put down. Because this kind of relationship takes time, I rate our possibilities here: _____

6. Freedom to talk isn't the only freedom. Freedom to "do" is also important. My friend is good about letting me participate in certain activities by myself. Yes_____ No_____
My friend also encourages me to enjoy friends of my own. Yes_____ No_____

The Unselfishness Questionnaire

1. The Bible says, "They that would have friends must show themselves friendly." Most of the time friendly people are not selfish people. They have the ability to get out of the way enough to concentrate on others. Does your friend have many friends? Yes___ No___

2. Few of us enjoy going out of our way to please the selfish. Is your friend the kind of person for whom other people like to do things? Yes___ No___

3. When you are planning something together, does your friend:

A. Ask you what you think first? ___
B. Tell you, "Here's what I think" and expect you to agree? ___
C. Pout if you get your way? ___

4. Are the words "thank you" heard often enough in your relationship? Genuine gratitude is another characteristic of the unselfish. On the grading scale 1 to 10 how do you grade your friend as a "thanker"? ___

5. How long has it been since your friend surprised you with some special little extra which seemed to say, "I think you're extra special?" ___

6. Some people are selfish because they were "spoiled" as children. They were given everything they wanted, almost as soon as they wanted it. Others had less than those around them and as a result, they are out to get their share.

Some home backgrounds were just right. In any way do you consider your friend "damaged" by too much or too little? Yes___No___Were you? Yes___ No___
Discuss together.

7. If the two of you had a job to do together and it was not your favorite thing, but it had to be done, would you expect:

A. You would end up doing more than your share. ___
B. Your friend would really pitch in. ___
C. You would divide it equally. ___

8. Which collection of words do you hear most often in your relationship?

"I" "Me" "My" "Mine" and the sounds of self-centered thinking. ___

"You" "Yours" "We" "Us" Our" "Ours" and the indicators of genuine "otherness" ___

The Mercy-Apology Questionnaire

1. Do you sometimes feel your friend is overcritical of others? Yes____ No____
And is your friend overcritical of you? Yes____ No____

2. Does your friend tend to gossip? Yes____ No____

3. Do you consider your friend generally positive about other people? Yes____ No____

4. When you tell your friend, "You're wrong," is the reaction likely to be (check one or more):
    defensive ____
    "I'm sorry" ____
    silent ____
    argumentative ____
    "I'll try to do better" ____
    angry ____
    grateful ____
    don't care ____

5. How long does it usually take your friend to apologize? ____

6. Does you friend tend to bring up past negatives in your relationship? Yes____ No____

7. Have you and your friend had an agreement on what to tell? How much to tell? Yes____ No____

Your Sexual IQ Test

1

Were you well trained early about sex? Yes____ No____

Did your parents give you adequate information as you needed it? Yes____ No____

On the scale of 1 to 10 (10 for perfect) grade your early sex education. ____

2

Do you know the correct words for the sex organs; for the different kinds of sexual activity? Yes____ No____

Do you know the meanings of the dirty words? Yes____ No____

How would you grade your sex vocabulary? (1 to 10) ____

3

Do you tend too much toward dirty stories, sexy jokes, shady humor? Yes____ No____

Are you overly interested in pornography, skin flicks, nude pictures, sex books? Yes____ No____

Put your sex attitudes up against the word "clean" and grade yourself 1 to 10. ____

4

Can you take a stand for what you think is right and make it stick? Yes____ No____

Would you let someone talk you into doing something you don't believe in? Yes____ No____

Grade yourself on your ability to do your own thing. (1 to 10) ____

5

Do you really have a feeling for the other person's feelings? Yes____ No____

Do you tend to pressure others too much to get your own way? Yes____ No____

Grade your overall respect for the beliefs, the morals, the standards of other people. (1 to 10) ____

6

Do you really care what your parents think? Yes____ No____

Would you ever do anything drastic to spite them, punish them, get even? Yes____ No____

How do you grade the climate between you and your parents? (1 to 10) ____

7

Are you acquainted with the laws of God (about sex) and have you decided what He expects of you personally? Yes____ No____

Do you think of God primarily as a punisher of evil? Yes____ No____

Or as a good friend who really cares about you? Yes____ No____

Grade your sense of responsibility to God (1 to 10) ____

8

Do you feel that you are normal in every way sexually? Yes____ No____

Do you look forward to building a happy sex life with the right person at the right time? Yes____ No____

For natural urges, self-control, healthy anticipation grade yourself (1 to 10) ____

The Money Questionnaire

Select the words which best describe your friend's attitude toward money:

careful ____
controlled ____
easy spender ____
happy-go-lucky ____
generous ____
careless ____
penurious ____
greedy ____
saving ____
selfish ____
extravagant ____
poor manager ____
stingy ____
too ambitious ____

Distance Questionnaire

Check the words and phrases which best fit your friend.
    Why risk it? ____
    Let's try it ____
    Sure, we can make it ____
    You might get hurt ____
    When in doubt, don't ____
    When in doubt, do ____
        overprotective ____
        daring ____
        adventuresome ____
        hesitant ____
        timid ____
        bold ____
        cautious ____
        curious ____

Listed here is a group of quotations from my Miscellany file. These are from people asking how their particular doubts, their wonderings might affect their future marriage. Check those you think need discussing between you.

____ "Sometimes Andy drinks too much. He says when we are married, he'll cut down. Do you think he will?"

____ "Melanie's folks don't like me, especially her mother. Is it all that important for a girl's parents to like the man she is going to marry?"

____ "My boy friend is O.K. with me when we're alone, but when any of his friends are around, he acts like he didn't even know me. What do you think is the matter?"

_____ "The one thing we wonder about is the way we fight all the time. My sister says not to worry, because she and her husband fight a lot and they're still together. But I'm not so sure. Wouldn't this get tiresome?"

_____ "I'm studying for my Master's in foreign languages. The man I'm engaged to didn't finish high school. I have to admit that when someone asks me where he went to college, I am somewhat embarrassed. How much priority should a couple give to common educational levels?"

_____ "Barbie has migraine headaches. Sometimes this worries me, because when I attended one of their family reunions it seemed all the women did was talk about how bad they felt. Should I tell Barbie?"

_____ "I never thought this would happen, but I think I am falling in love with Milton. He is in the Air Corps, which creates a problem. I was brought up in a pacifist home where the military was always put down. I have honestly tried to get over this, but it is very hard for me. Milton is wild about flying and he plans to stay in for a career. Neither one of us knows what to do. Can you help us?"

_____ "I am going with a man thirteen years older. My mother says that is too much difference, because he will be an old man when I am still young. She says she has seen it happen too often and I will be sorry if I marry him. Is that right?"

(Read the next two together).
_____ "My fiancee says she does not want to have children. Because the world is so mixed up, she says it wouldn't be fair to bring children into it. But my family has meant a lot to me and I have looked forward to having a family of my

150

own."

That statement comes from the male side. Now here is another, more familiar:

_____ "Craig is number one in our class, a real brain, but here is our problem. He says he never wants children and I know what he is thinking. He is afraid children would get in the way and take too much time. The truth is children are one of the big things with me, including other people's children. But mostly having children of my own. Do you think I should marry him and hope he will get over it?"

_____ "The man I am going with is more of a gentleman than anyone I've ever known. But there is one thing that bothers me. He is twenty-seven years old and still lives with his mother. In almost everything he does, it is like he checks with her. We have discussed marriage some, and if it gets more serious, do you feel I have anything to worry about?"

_____ "In our family my father was definitely head of the house and we all knew it and liked it. Even my mother liked it. But with Marshall and me, it's almost the exact opposite. It seems as if he leaves everything up to me. I don't mind sharing responsibility, but do you think it could ever work for a woman to take complete charge of everything?"

The Fun Questionnaire

1. I think my friend spends too much time on _____ and as I see it, this could develop into a problem between us. Yes____ No____

2. I believe there is a possibility we spend too much time with other people. Yes____ No____
   Not enough time. Yes____ No____
   About right. Yes____ No____

3. Here are some things we have never tried which I think might be fun for both of us: _____, _____, _____.

FUN AND YOUR BASIC ATTITUDES

Are they right, those who say that all the world can be divided into two groups, Necrophiles and Biophiles? Necrophiles are the down-beat people. These are the lovers of doom, the pessimistic. Their thoughts turn to the dark and "Necro," meaning death, puts them on the side of, "Oh, isn't it awful?"

Biophiles move to the light. They are up with people, up with life, up with what's about to happen, expecting a miracle, optimistic.

Although it may be oversimplifying to divide the world and everyone in it by two categories, if you had to limit your choice to these two definitions, how would you rate your friend? Necrophile _____ Biophile _____

How do you rate yourself? Necrophile _____ Biophile _____

152

HUMOR

One indicator of people's fun philosophy is the humor they find attractive. Some get their jollies putting other people down, embarrassing others, ridiculing. These can be tough people to live with over the years.

Others include a shady touch in their fun. They get their laughs from the banal; the bawdy, the sometimes vulgar. West Point Cadets have a prayer: "Lord, if I can't be funny and clean, help me to only be clean."

Using the scale one to ten
For kindness in humor I rate my friend ____
My rating ____
Against the prayer of the West Point cadets, I rate my friend's humor ____
Mine ____

THEOLOGY

Theology is a combination of the two words, "Theos" and "logos," meaning thoughts of God. Our theology can make a major difference in our ability to have fun.

Which of these words do you most often associate with God?

joy ____
light ____
gladness ____
likeable ____
friend ____
severe ____
judgment ____
stern ____
strict ____
authoritarian ____

Questions with Many Answers: What Do You Say?

When I was in college we had a professor of philosophy who would tease us with the test question: "Define the universe and give three examples."

Some questions coming my way are like that. There is **no** pat answer. Many of these are better discussed **than** jammed into a single letter or answered in a short time.

Listed here are questions in this category. Some can **be** answered several ways. This is a questionnaire where **I** hope you and your friend may make mecca to your favorite talking place and bend each other's ear.

Do you think God has one person in the whole world **who** is right for me?

Is there such a thing as love at first sight?

Is it possible to be in love with two people at the **same** time?

What do you think about black-white marriage?

What is the best age for marriage?

Is computer dating ever a good thing?

If I don't want to go with someone anymore, how can **I** tell them?

Isn't it true a man and woman can communicate without words?

154

If prayer draws two people closer in every way, is it wise to pray together when you know you can't get married for a while?

Do you think it is possible that you might quit growing in a relationship if you are having sex?

After you are married, how long should you wait to have children?

Should a woman work even if the couple has children?

Does it ever work for the man to stay home, do the housework, raise the children, while the wife earns the living?

If I am religious and my fiance is an agnostic, how could we have a good marriage?

My church says I should not marry, because I have been divorced. But I am in love. Should I do it anyway?

And now for the big one—
   What does it really mean to say:
     Marriage is not so much
     finding the right person
     As it is being the right person.